WEAPONS
& TACTICS

A HANDBOOK ON PERSONAL EVANGELISM

JIM WILSON

canonpress
Moscow, Idaho

Jim Wilson, *Weapons & Tactics: A Handbook on Personal Evangelism*
Copyright © 2012 by James I. Wilson

Published by Canon Press, P.O. Box 8729, Moscow, ID 83843
800.488.2034 | www.canonpress.com

Cover design by David Dalbey.
Interior design by Laura Storm.
Printed in the United States of America.

Library of Congress Cataloging-in-Publication Data
Wilson, James I.
 Weapons & tactics : a handbook on personal evangelism / Jim Wilson.
    p. cm.
 ISBN 978-1-59128-115-3
 1. Evangelistic work. 2. Spiritual warfare. I. Title. II. Title: Weapons and tactics.
 BV3790.W4945 2012
 269'.2--dc23
                                    2012001479

12 13 14 15 16 17 18 19 20   9 8 7 6 5 4 3 2 1

FOR KEN & LIZ KORKOW,

who have stayed in the
front of the fight

Also by the author

Principles of War

How to Be Free from Bitterness

Christ in Relationships DVD

CONTENTS

PART TWO: TACTICS

PREFACE

W*eapons and Tactics* was written to give methods for implementing the principles laid out in my earlier book *Principles of War*. This book has many scriptural passages and some examples. I hope the scriptural quotations alone will hit you hard. I have quoted Scripture extensively, and have drawn your attention to certain parts of those passages by means of italics. The italics are not my attempt to make Scripture stronger, but are simply a way of pointing to what the Lord is saying to all of us.

The first half of this book speaks of the *weapons* that God has given us for the part of the spiritual war related to evangelism. The second half is on the use of these weapons, that is, the *tactics* of evangelism. It follows the principles of war, but on a personal level, illustrating methods for putting those principles into effect. I would encourage you to read *Principles of War* as preparation for this study, as what I have written presupposes that.

You may have already learned and practiced much of this. If any of it is new and fresh to you, please pray that God will give you an opportunity to practice what you have learned right away. Do not wait to finish the book. There is no substitute for obedience now.

There is a simple command in Ephesians 5 which, if followed, would make all of the evangelism described in this book both normal and easy:

> Be filled with the Spirit, speaking to yourselves in psalms and hymns and spiritual songs, singing and making melody in your heart to the Lord, giving thanks always for all things unto God and the Father in the name of our Lord Jesus Christ, submitting yourselves one to another in the fear of God. (Eph. 5:18b–21, KJV)

Keep on being filled with the Spirit. May God use you greatly as you participate in this great war that God launched to liberate the souls of men from death and from the fear of death. If you find anything biblically false, certainly write to me.

I am grateful to the staff at Community Christian Ministries who have put up with me and helped put this book together. *Particular thanks should go to Lisa Just for her essential labors in assembling this material.* I would also thank Debbie Hulbert, Jen Miller, Naomi Adams, Colleen McGarry, Heather Torosyan, and Amy Bakken. Thanks also to Tom Banks and the many other proofreaders who offered their kind suggestions.

In the Lord Jesus Christ,
JIM WILSON
January 2012

INTRODUCTION

Men and women are never the enemy in the spiritual war. We have only one enemy—Satan. We fight him and those spiritual powers in league with him.

Finally, be strong in the Lord and in His mighty power. Put on the full armor of God so that you can take your stand against the devil's schemes. For our struggle is not against flesh and blood, but against the *rulers, against the authorities, against the powers of this dark world and against the spiritual forces of evil in the heavenly realms.* Therefore put on the full armor of God, so that when the day of evil comes, you may be able to stand your ground, and after you have done everything, to stand. Stand firm then, with the belt of truth buckled around your waist, with the breastplate of righteousness in place, and with your feet fitted with the readiness that comes from the gospel of peace. In addition to all this, take up the shield of faith, with which you can extinguish all the flaming arrows of the evil one. Take the helmet of salvation and the sword of the Spirit, which is the word of God. And pray in the Spirit on all occasions with all kinds of prayers

and requests. With this in mind, be alert and always keep
on praying for all the saints. (Eph. 6:10–18)

The unsaved are captives of the Enemy. We fight to deliver
them from his power. They are what the war is *over*—they
are the contested territory.

Don't have anything to do with foolish and stupid arguments, because you know they produce quarrels. And the
Lord's servant must not quarrel; instead, *he must be kind to
everyone*, able to teach, not resentful. *Those who oppose him he
must gently instruct, in the hope that God will grant them repentance* leading them to a knowledge of the truth, and that they
will come to their senses *and escape from the trap of the devil,
who has taken them captive to do his will.* (2 Tim. 2:23–26)

These people are slaves to sin, and we are to seek their
liberation.

But thanks be to God that, though *you used to be slaves to sin*,
you wholeheartedly obeyed the form of teaching to which
you were entrusted. (Rom. 6:17)

When you were slaves to sin, you were free from the control
of righteousness. (Rom. 6:20)

Those enslaved to sin are not our enemies. At the funda-
mental level, we do not fight them; we are fighting to *rescue*
them. The gospel is therefore the only true liberation front.

PART I

WEAPONS

CHAPTER I

THE WEAPONS
of Our Warfare

If this is a war, then there must be weapons. What are those weapons?

> For though we live in the world, we do not wage war as the world does. The weapons we fight with are not the weapons of the world. On the contrary, they have divine power to demolish strongholds. We demolish arguments and every pretension that sets itself up against the knowledge of God, and we take captive every thought to make it obedient to Christ. (2 Cor. 10:3–5)

The world wages war with weapons that kill and destroy, whether they be clubs, arrows, swords, rifles, bombs, missiles, starvation, or chemical, biological, and atomic weapons. The history of warfare is filled with pillaging, looting, raping, torture, murder, and prostitution. Secular warfare is motivated by envy, covetousness, pride, glory, fear, vengeance, patriotism, anger, hatred, and defense of home. There are legitimate reasons for war (there was, after all, war in heaven), but most of the warfare in this world is simply carnal.

But the weapons we fight with are not the weapons of the world. These are our weapons: *the Gospel* (1 Cor. 15:1–5), *the grace of God*, *the mercy of God*, *the blood of Christ* (Rev. 12:11), *the name of Jesus Christ* (Acts 4:12), *the Holy Spirit* (in divine power, 2 Peter 1:3, in conviction, John 16:7–11, in prayer, Ephesians 6:18, in preaching, Acts 8:4), *the fruit of the Spirit* (Galatians 5:22–23), *humility* (Eph. 4:2), *the Sword of the Spirit* (Eph. 6:17), *terror* (Lk. 21:26–27), and *our testimony* (Rev. 12:11). I will devote a chapter to a discussion of each of these.

Our weapons are not carnal weapons. Our motives for taking up these weapons should be love for God and love for man (our neighbors, brothers, and enemies).

CHAPTER 2

THE GOSPEL

In order to understand the weapons of our spiritual warfare, we must begin with the gospel.

> Now, brothers, I want to remind you of the gospel I preached to you, which you received and on which you have taken your stand. *By this gospel you are saved,* if you hold firmly to the word I preached to you. Otherwise, you have believed in vain. For what I received I passed on to you as of first importance: *that Christ died for our sins according to the Scriptures, that He was buried, that He was raised on the third day according to the Scriptures,* that He appeared to Peter, then to the Twelve. After that, He appeared to more than five hundred of the brothers at the same time, most of whom are still living, though some have fallen asleep. Then He appeared to James, then to all the apostles, and last of all He appeared to me also, as to one abnormally born. (1 Cor. 15:1–8)

> Then He opened their minds so they could understand the Scriptures. He told them, "This is what is written: *The Christ will suffer and rise from the dead on the third day, and repentance and forgiveness of sins will be preached in His name to all nations,*

beginning at Jerusalem. You are witnesses of these things. I
am going to send you what My Father has promised; but stay
in the city until you have been clothed with power from on
high." (Lk. 24:45–49)

"Men of Israel, listen to this: Jesus of Nazareth was a man
accredited by God to you by miracles, wonders and signs,
which God did among you through Him, as you yourselves
know. This man was handed over to you by God's set purpose and foreknowledge; and you, with the help of wicked
men, *put Him to death by nailing Him to the cross. But God
raised Him from the dead*, freeing Him from the agony of
death, because it was impossible for death to keep its hold
on Him . . . Brothers, I can tell you confidently that the
patriarch David died and was buried, and his tomb is here
to this day. But he was a prophet and knew that God had
promised him on oath that he would place one of his de-
scendants on his throne. Seeing what was ahead, he spoke
of *the resurrection of the Christ*, that He was not abandoned
to the grave, nor did His body see decay. God has raised this
Jesus to life, and we are all witnesses of the fact. Exalted to
the right hand of God, He has received from the Father the
promised Holy Spirit and has poured out what you now see
and hear. For David did not ascend to heaven, and yet he
said, 'The Lord said to my Lord: "Sit at my right hand until
I make your enemies a footstool for your feet."' Therefore let
all Israel be assured of this: *God has made this Jesus, whom you
crucified, both Lord and Christ*." When the people heard this,
they were cut to the heart and said to Peter and the other
apostles, "Brothers, what shall we do?" Peter replied, "Repent and be baptized, every one of you, in the name of Jesus
Christ for the forgiveness of your sins. And you will receive
the gift of the Holy Spirit. The promise is for you and your
children and for all who are far off—for all whom the Lord
our God will call." With many other words he warned them;

and he pleaded with them, "Save yourselves from this corrupt generation." Those who accepted his message were baptized, and about three thousand were added to their number that day. (Acts 2:22–24, 29–41)

"You know the message God sent to the people of Israel, telling the good news of peace through *Jesus Christ, who is Lord of all.* You know what has happened throughout Judea, beginning in Galilee after the baptism that John preached— how God anointed Jesus of Nazareth with the Holy Spirit and power, and how He went around doing good and healing all who were under the power of the devil, because God was with Him. We are witnesses of everything He did in the country of the Jews and in Jerusalem. *They killed Him by hanging Him on a tree, but God raised Him from the dead on the third day* and caused Him to be seen. He was not seen by all the people, but by witnesses whom God had already chosen—by us who ate and drank with Him after He rose from the dead. He commanded us to preach to the people and to testify that He is the one whom God appointed as judge of the living and the dead. All the prophets testify about Him that *everyone who believes in Him receives forgiveness of sins* through His name." While Peter was still speaking these words, the Holy Spirit came on all who heard the message. (Acts 10:36–44)

These Scripture selections were chosen to highlight the truth which forms the essential part of the gospel. This minimum of truth that we must maintain and proclaim is *the deity of Jesus Christ, His death for our sins, His burial,* and *His resurrection.* Whenever the gospel is preached, this should be in the message.

Man's proper response to this gospel is to repent and believe. The result is forgiveness of sins and everlasting life.

CHAPTER 3

THE GRACE

of God

What moved God to offer this gospel to us? The answer is the grace of God, which we in turn wield as weapons in this warfare.

> Out of his fullness *we have all received grace* in place of grace already given. For the law was given through Moses; grace and truth came through Jesus Christ. (Jn. 1:16–17)

> So too, at the present time there is a remnant *chosen by grace*. And if by grace, then it cannot be based on works; if it were, grace would no longer be grace. (Rom. 11:5–6)

> Let your conversation be always *full of grace*, seasoned with salt, so that you may know how to answer everyone. (Col. 4:6)

> The law was brought in so that the trespass might increase. But where sin increased, *grace increased all the more.* (Rom. 5:20)

But he said to me, "My *grace is sufficient* for you, for my power is made perfect in weakness." Therefore I will boast all the more gladly about my weaknesses, so that Christ's power may rest on me. (2 Cor. 12:9)

Grace is a gift from God that provides what man cannot provide for himself—righteousness, forgiveness, and power. God is not stingy with His grace. He gives it in *great quantities.*

In him we have redemption through his blood, the forgiveness of sins, in accordance with *the riches of God's grace that he lavished on us.* (Eph. 1:7–8a)

But because of his great love for us, God, who is rich in mercy, made us alive with Christ even when we were dead in transgressions—it is by grace you have been saved. And God raised us up with Christ and seated us with him in the heavenly realms in Christ Jesus, in order that in the coming ages he might show *the incomparable riches of his grace,* expressed in his kindness to us in Christ Jesus. For it is by grace you have been saved, through faith—and this is not from yourselves, it is the gift of God—not by works, so that no one can boast. (Eph 2:4–9)

The apostle Paul received grace *from* God in order to preach the grace *of* God. We also need grace in order to preach grace.

Through him we received grace and apostleship to call all the Gentiles to the obedience that comes from faith for his name's sake. (Rom. 1:5)

Surely you have heard about the administration of God's grace that was given to me for you, that is, the mystery made known to me by revelation, as I have already written briefly. In reading this, then, you will be able to understand my insight into the mystery of Christ, which was not made known to people in other generations as it has now been revealed by the Spirit to God's holy apostles and prophets. (Eph. 2:3–5)

CHAPTER 4

THE MERCY

of God

God has not only been gracious to us, but also merciful.

> But because of his great love for us, *God, who is rich in mercy*, made us alive with Christ even when we were dead in transgressions. (Eph. 2:4–5a)

> Praise be to the God and Father of our Lord Jesus Christ! In *his great mercy* he has given us new birth into a living hope through the resurrection of Jesus Christ from the dead. (1 Pet. 1:3)

> *He saved us,* not because of righteous things we had done, but *because of his mercy.* (Tit. 3:5)

> But the wisdom that comes from heaven is first of all pure; then peace-loving, considerate, submissive, full of mercy and good fruit, impartial and sincere. (Jas. 3:17)

Mercy is the work of God. It also comes in quantities, just like grace does. The Bible describes God's mercy as rich, great, and full.

We are to show mercy to the people we are preaching to: doubters, those in the fire, those who are caught up in sin. It must be genuine mercy, not feigned.

> *Be merciful* to those who doubt; save others by snatching them from the fire; to others show mercy, mixed with fear—hating even the clothing stained by corrupted flesh. (Jude 22–23)

There is a basic difference between grace and mercy. Grace is *receiving* something wonderful which we do *not* deserve (forgiveness of sins and everlasting life). Mercy is *not receiving* what we *do* deserve (the lake of fire).

CHAPTER 5

THE BLOOD
of Christ

As Scripture describes it, another great weapon in our arsenal is the blood of Jesus Christ.

> The great dragon was hurled down—that ancient serpent called the devil, or Satan, who leads the whole world astray. He was hurled to the earth, and his angels with him. Then I heard a loud voice in heaven say: "Now have come the salvation and the power and the kingdom of our God, and the authority of his Messiah. For the accuser of our brothers and sisters, who accuses them before our God day and night, has been hurled down. They triumphed over him by the blood of the Lamb and by the word of their testimony; they did not love their lives so much as to shrink from death." (Rev. 12:9–11)

"They" are "our brothers" (v. 10). The "him" they triumphed over is "Satan" (v. 9). Their weapon was the blood of the Lamb, the blood of the Lord Jesus Christ.

The blood of Christ works in our salvation, our redemption, and for our continual cleansing:

And from Jesus Christ, who is the faithful witness, the first-born from the dead, and the ruler of the kings of the earth. *To Him who loves us and has freed us from our sins by His blood,* and has made us to be a kingdom and priests to serve His God and Father—to Him be glory and power for ever and ever! Amen. (Rev. 1:5–6)

God presented Him as a sacrifice of *atonement, through faith in His blood.* He did this to demonstrate his justice, because in His forbearance He had left the sins committed beforehand unpunished. (Rom. 3:25)

Since *we have now been justified by His blood,* how much more shall we be saved from God's wrath through Him! (Rom. 5:9)

For you know that it was not with perishable things such as silver or gold that you were redeemed from the empty way of life handed down to you from your forefathers, but *with the precious blood of Christ,* a lamb without blemish or defect. (1 Pet. 1:18–19)

But if we walk in the light, as he is in the light, we have fellowship with one another, and *the blood of Jesus,* His Son, purifies us from all sin. (1 Jn. 1:7)

He entered the Most Holy Place once for all *by his own blood,* having obtained eternal redemption. (Heb. 9:12b)

How much more, then, will the blood of Christ, who through the eternal Spirit offered himself unblemished to God, cleanse our consciences from acts that lead to death, so that we may serve the living God! . . . In fact, the law requires that nearly everything be cleansed with blood, and without the shedding of blood there is no forgiveness. (Heb. 9:14, 22)

So the blood of Christ is clearly a weapon. By the shedding of His blood, Christ saved the believers, and through His blood they overcame Satan. "The blood of the Lamb" is not just a phrase to say. It is not a mantra. It is the bloody death of the Lord Jesus Christ that overcomes, not the phraseology. Hebrews 2:14 says it this way:

> Since the children have flesh and blood, He too shared in their *humanity so that by His death* He might destroy him who holds the power of death—that is, the devil.

Focus on the second phrase: "so that by His death," that is, by the blood of the Lamb, "He might destroy him who holds the power of death." We use this truth by *believing* it. When we believe this, we pray and preach the death of Christ, and we are not just saying words. When we believe it, we are wielding it.

CHAPTER 6

THE NAME

of Christ

God has granted us a great range of powerful weapons. Another is the name of Jesus.

"Therefore let all Israel be assured of this: God has made *this Jesus, whom you crucified, both Lord and Christ.*". . . Peter replied, "Repent and be baptized, every one of you, in the *name of Jesus Christ* for the forgiveness of your sins. And you will receive the gift of the Holy Spirit. The promise is for you and your children and for all who are far off—for all whom the Lord our God will call." (Acts 2:36–39)

They had Peter and John brought before them and began to question them: "By what power or what *name* did you do this?". . ."Then know this, you and all the people of Israel: It is by the *name* of Jesus Christ of Nazareth, whom you crucified but whom God raised from the dead, that this man stands before you healed". . . they called them in again and commanded them not to speak or teach at all in the name Jesus. (Acts 4:7, 10, 18)

Now, Lord, consider their threats and enable your servants to speak your word with great boldness. Stretch out your hand to heal and perform miraculous signs and wonders through the name of your holy servant Jesus. (Acts 4:29–30)

So Saul stayed with them and moved about freely in Jerusalem, speaking boldly in the *name* of the Lord. (Acts 9:28)

It is strange to me that the name of Jesus Christ is used much more by unbelievers than by believers. Unbelievers use His name mockingly, irreverently, and thoughtlessly. They use it in vain. Believers do not want to use Christ's name in vain. Instead, they do not use it at all. However, it is absolutely necessary to use Christ's name in our presentation of the gospel.

Salvation is found in no one else, for there is *no other name* under heaven given to men by which we must be saved (Acts 4:12)

Without His name no one can be saved.

Many years ago I came aboard an aircraft carrier in the East China Sea by high-wire from another carrier. I arrived at noon, just in time for the meal in the wardroom. I did not know anyone on the ship. I started to take a chair at one of the tables, next to a lieutenant. He looked at me and said, "That seat's saved." So I took the next chair. Soon an ensign came in, sat in the saved seat, and immediately started talking to me. He was griping about the communication officer, a lieutenant commander, who was his boss. He told me about all of his faults and how poor an officer he was. I asked the ensign about his own relationships with the enlisted men. I asked him in detail. After he had answered my questions, I said to him, "You are going to be the same kind of lieutenant commander your boss is."

"I guess you're right," he said. "What's the solution?"

I replied, "Do you really want to know?"

He said that he did.

I answered, "Jesus Christ." He knew I was not swearing.

"Would you tell me about him? I have always wanted to know about Jesus. My parents are both atheists. They would not let me go to Sunday school."

I told him about Jesus. He received Christ a few weeks later.

> "We gave you strict orders not to teach in this *name*," he said. "Yet you have filled Jerusalem with your teaching and are determined to make us guilty of this man's blood." (Acts 5:28)

> His speech persuaded them. They called the apostles in and had them flogged. Then they ordered them not to speak in the *name* Jesus, and let them go. (Acts 5:40)

> All those who heard him were astonished and asked, "Isn't he the man who raised havoc in Jerusalem among those who call on this *name*? And hasn't he come here to take them as prisoners to the chief priests?" (Acts 9:21)

There has always been opposition to the use of the Lord's name. The name and identity of Jesus Christ are foremost in the gospel.

> But these are written that you may believe that Jesus is the Christ, the Son of God, and that by believing you may have life in his *name*. (Jn. 20:31)

CHAPTER 7

THE HOLY SPIRIT

There is so much in Scripture about the relationship of the Holy Spirit to our presentation of the gospel that we will take up the subject in sections.

IN DIVINE POWER

I baptize you with water for repentance. But after me comes one who is more powerful than I, whose sandals I am not worthy to carry. He will baptize you with the Holy Spirit and fire. (Mt. 3:11)

All of them were filled with the Holy Spirit and began to speak in other tongues as the Spirit enabled them. (Acts 2:4)

Paul, a servant of Christ Jesus, called to be an apostle and set apart for the gospel of God—the gospel he promised beforehand through his prophets in the Holy Scriptures regarding his Son, who as to his human nature was a descendant of David, and who through the Spirit of holiness was declared with power to be the Son of God by his resurrection from the dead: Jesus Christ our Lord. Through him and for his name's sake, we received grace and apostleship to call people from among all the Gentiles to the obedience that comes from faith. (Rom. 1:1–5)

His divine power has given us everything we need for life and godliness through our knowledge of him who called us by his own glory and goodness. (2 Pet. 1:3)

For this reason I kneel before the Father, from whom his whole family in heaven and on earth derives its name. I pray that out of his glorious riches he may strengthen you with power through his Spirit in your inner being, so that Christ may dwell in your hearts through faith. And I pray that you, being rooted and established in love, may have power, together with all the saints, to grasp how wide and long and high and deep is the love of Christ, and to know this love that surpasses knowledge—that you may be filled to the measure of all the fullness of God. Now to him who is able to do immeasurably more than all we ask or imagine, according to his power that is at work within us, to him be glory in the church and in Christ Jesus throughout all generations, for ever and ever! Amen. (Eph. 3:14–21)

I pray also that the eyes of your heart may be enlightened in order that you may know the hope to which he has called you, the riches of his glorious inheritance in the saints, and his incomparably great power for us who believe. That power is like the working of his mighty strength, which he exerted in Christ when he raised him from the dead and seated him at his right hand in the heavenly realms, far above all rule and authority, power and dominion, and every title that can be given, not only in the present age but also in the one to come. (Eph. 1:18–21)

God's divine power is available to us in proclaiming the gospel. It is His power that is at work within us, through the Holy Spirit who dwells in us.

IN CONVICTION

> Nevertheless I tell you the truth. It is to your advantage that
> I go away; for if I do not go away, the Helper will not come
> to you; but if I depart, I will send Him to you. And when He
> has come, *He will convict* the world of sin, and of righteous-
> ness, and of judgment: of sin, because they do not believe in
> Me; of righteousness, because I go to My Father and you see
> Me no more. (Jn. 16:7–10, NKJV)

The Helper, the Holy Spirit, convicts men of sin. This
conviction is one of the states that precede repentance.

IN PRAYER

> And *pray in the Spirit* on all occasions with all kinds of prayers
> and requests. With this in mind, be alert and always keep on
> praying for all the saints. Pray also for me, that whenever I
> open my mouth, words may be given me so *that I will fear-
> lessly make known the mystery of the gospel.* (Eph. 6:18–19)

Praying for saints and sinners is a major part of the
proclamation of the gospel. What are we to pray? For
the saints:

> For this reason, since the day we heard about you, *we have
> not stopped praying* for you. We continually ask God to fill
> you with the knowledge of his will through all the wisdom
> and understanding that the Spirit gives, so that you may
> live a life worthy of the Lord and please him in every way:
> bearing fruit in every good work, growing in the knowledge
> of God, being strengthened with all power according to his
> glorious might so that you may have great endurance and
> patience, and giving joyful thanks to the Father, who has
> qualified you to share in the inheritance of his holy people
> in the kingdom of light. (Col. 1:9–12)

And *this is my prayer*: that your love may abound more and more in knowledge and depth of insight, so that you may be able to discern what is best and may be pure and blameless for the day of Christ, filled with the fruit of righteousness that comes through Jesus Christ—to the glory and praise of God. (Phil. 1:9–11)

For this reason I kneel before the Father, from whom his whole family in heaven and on earth derives its name. *I pray* that out of his glorious riches he may strengthen you with power through *his Spirit* your inner being, *so that Christ may dwell in your hearts through faith*. And *I pray* that you, being rooted and established in love, may have *power*, together with all the saints, to grasp how wide and long and high and deep is the love of Christ, and to know this love that surpasses knowledge—that you may be filled to the measure of all the fullness of God (Eph. 3:14–19)

When he saw the crowds, he had compassion on them, because they were harassed and helpless, like sheep without a shepherd. Then he said to his disciples, "The harvest is plentiful but the workers are few. *Ask the Lord of the harvest*, therefore, to send out workers into his harvest field." (Mt. 9:36–38)

For sinners:

I urge, then, first of all, that petitions, prayers, intercession and thanksgiving be made for all people—for kings and all those in authority, that we may live peaceful and quiet lives in all godliness and holiness. This is good, and pleases God our Savior, who wants all people to be saved and to come to a knowledge of the truth. (1 Tim. 2:1–4)

While they were stoning him, Stephen prayed, "Lord Jesus, receive my spirit." Then he fell on his knees and cried out,

"Lord, do not hold this sin against them." When he had said this, he fell asleep. (Acts 7:59–60)

Notice that the prayers for saints in evangelism occur more frequently than the prayers for sinners.

IN PREACHING

Then Peter, *filled with the Holy Spirit*, said to them: "Rulers and elders of the people! If we are being called to account today for an act of kindness shown to a cripple and are asked how he was healed, then know this, you and all the people of Israel: It is by the name of Jesus Christ of Nazareth, whom you crucified but whom God raised from the dead, that this man stands before you healed. He is 'the stone you builders rejected, which has become the capstone.'" (Acts 4:8–11)

It is possible to preach the gospel without being filled with the Holy Spirit. It is better to be scared enough to pray for a Holy Spirit kind of boldness. With Holy Spirit boldness comes *power.*

CHAPTER 8

THE FRUIT

of the Spirit

The fruit of the Spirit is true evidence that someone has been of the Holy Spirit, has been by the Holy Spirit, or has the Spirit. It is possible to be baptized "into the name of the Lord Jesus" but not be baptized into the body of Christ by the Holy Spirit. Water baptism is meant as a sign of salvation, but it does not save.

The fruit of the Spirit is essential to evangelism. It is part of our arsenal of weapons which are not carnal. Without this fruit it is impossible to preach and pray in the Holy Spirit.

The fruit of the Spirit is given to each new Christian at the time he receives Christ. It is the primary evidence of life in Christ. The Christian has it, and he is commanded to *express* it. If someone does not have the fruit of the Spirit, he is not a Christian. If he has it and does not express it, he is a disobedient Christian.

LOVE

> But the fruit of the Spirit is *love*, joy, peace, patience, kindness, goodness, faithfulness. (Gal. 5:22)

> A new command I give you: *Love one another.* As I have loved you, so you must love one another. By this all men will know that you are my disciples, if you love one another. (Jn. 13:34–35)

We are told to love our brothers in Christ. This love tells all of the non-brothers that we are followers of Jesus Christ. This is indirect evangelism. *"Love your neighbor* as yourself" (Mt. 22:39b).

Our neighbor may not be a Christian. We are to love him because he is a neighbor.

> But I tell you who hear me: *Love your enemies*, do good to those who hate you, bless those who curse you, pray for those who mistreat you. If someone strikes you on one cheek, turn to him the other also. If someone takes your cloak, do not stop him from taking your tunic. Give to everyone who asks you, and if anyone takes what belongs to you, do not demand it back. Do to others as you would have them do to you. If you love those who love you, what credit is that to you? Even "sinners" love those who love them. And if you do good to those who are good to you, what credit is that to you? Even "sinners" do that. And if you lend to those from whom you expect repayment, what credit is that to you? Even "sinners" lend to "sinners," expecting to be repaid in full. *But love your enemies, do good to them, and lend to them without expecting to get anything back.* Then your reward will be great, and you will be sons of the Most High, because *he* is kind to the ungrateful and wicked. Be merciful, just as your Father is merciful. (Lk. 6:27–36)

We are also to love our enemies. Jesus tells us to love them and to express that love in these ways:

1. Do good to them.
2. Bless them.
3. Pray for them.
4. Give to them.
5. Lend to them.

Jesus does not tell us why to love our enemies, only that by doing so we will be imitating our Father. Romans 5:10 tells us what happened when *we* were God's enemies:

> For if, when we were God's enemies, we were reconciled to him through the death of his Son, how much more, having been reconciled, shall we be saved through his life! (Rom. 5:10)

When we were enemies of God, He loved us. What was the result? We were saved. That is why we are to love our enemies—for their salvation.

When speaking at men's conferences, I often ask this question: "How many of you came to the Father through 1) mass evangelism, 2) a local church, 3) family, 4) reading the Bible, 5) reading books, or 6) a friend?" Several men raise their hands for each of these. Then I ask, "How many of you received Christ because someone loved you?" Nearly everyone raises their hand. The greatest positive emotion in the world is love, and the greatest love in the world is the love of the Father.

> Whoever does not love does not know God, because *God is love.* This is how God showed His love among us: He sent His one and only Son into the world that we might live through Him. This is love: not that we loved God, but that

He loved us and sent His Son as an atoning sacrifice for our sins. (1 Jn. 4:8–10)

The greatest expression of love in the history of the world is the death of Jesus. So when we proclaim His death, we should do it with *love* for the person we are speaking to. Presenting the gospel to someone without loving him makes the good news sound like bad news. Even if you are knocking on a stranger's door or sitting next to someone you do not know on a plane, decide to love him from your heart before you open your mouth. If God loved the world, then we can love one person through His grace.

Here is how Paul expressed loving and identifying with people:

> Though I am free and belong to no man, *I make myself a slave to everyone, to win as many as possible.* To the Jews I became like a Jew, to win the Jews. To those under the law I became like one under the law (though I myself am not under the law), so as to win those under the law. To those not having the law I became like one not having the law (though I am not free from God's law but am under Christ's law), so as to win those not having the law. To the weak I became weak, to win the weak. I have become all things to all men so that by all possible means I might save some. (1 Cor. 9:19–22)

JOY

> But the fruit of the Spirit is love, *joy*, peace, patience, kindness, goodness, faithfulness. (Gal. 5:22)

Joy is difficult to contain. It overflows. Here is an example of what happened when David's sin caused him to lose his joy:

Restore to me the *joy* of Your salvation and grant me a willing spirit, to sustain me. Then I will teach transgressors Your ways, and *sinners will turn back to You.* (Ps. 51:12–13)

Joy is attractive. When it is restored, sinners are converted. Before I received Christ, I was not happy, but I wanted to be. I saw men who seemed to be happy. They were not happy; they were *joyful.* I did not know the difference, but I wanted what they had.

If you are a Christian and are not joyful, you are under the chastening of the Lord because of unconfessed sin. Confess your sins and *your life of joy will be a witness.*

Now no chastening for the present seemeth to be joyous, but grievous: nevertheless afterward it yieldeth the peaceable fruit of righteousness unto them which are exercised thereby. (Heb. 12:11, KJV)

Surely God is my salvation; I will trust and not be afraid. The LORD, the LORD, is my strength and my song; He has become my salvation. *With joy you will draw water from the wells of salvation.* (Is. 12:2–3)

PEACE

But the fruit of the Spirit is love, joy, *peace*, patience, kindness, goodness, faithfulness. (Gal. 5:22)

When you enter a house, first say, "*Peace* to this house." If a man of peace is there, your peace will rest on him; if not, it will return to you. (Lk. 10:5–6)

Therefore, since we have been justified through faith, we have *peace* with God through our Lord Jesus Christ. (Rom. 5:1)

Peace with God is the result of justification. The fruit of the Spirit is peace, and the first words we are to use in house-to-house evangelism are "*Peace* to this house."

We fight the spiritual war with the weapon of *peace*. Jesus said to Pilate,

> My kingdom is not of this world. If it were, my servants would fight to prevent my arrest by the Jews. But now my kingdom is from another place. (Jn. 18:36)

We do not use weapons of physical war in evangelism, and that is good. But we also do not consistently present the good news in peace, which we should. Many evangelists present the gospel with a belligerent attitude. Do not do that. The message of the gospel is reconciliation with God and peace for the world. The Prince of Peace went to the cross peacefully. The news of His death and resurrection should be presented *peacefully*.

> *Grace and peace to you* from God our Father and the Lord Jesus Christ. (2 Cor. 1:2)

PATIENCE

> But the fruit of the Spirit is love, joy, peace, *patience*, kindness, goodness, faithfulness. (Gal. 5:22)

Patience in evangelism starts with God:

> The Lord is not slow in keeping his promise, as some understand slowness. *He is patient with you, not wanting anyone to perish, but everyone to come to repentance.* (2 Pet. 3:9)

We think God is slow when He is just patient. He tells us to wait patiently too, because that means the salvation of more people:

Be patient, then, brothers, until the Lord's coming. See how the farmer waits for the land to yield its valuable crop and how *patient* he is for the autumn and spring rains. You too, be patient and stand firm, because the Lord's coming is near. (Jas. 5:7–8)

In personal evangelism there is a time to plow, to disc, and to harrow the ground. There is a time to plant. There is a time to wait for the autumn and spring rains. Then there is a time to harvest. Everything prior to the harvest requires patience.

When the harvest is ripe, patience is no longer needed:

Do you not say, "Four months more and then the harvest"? I tell you, open your eyes and look at the fields! They are ripe for harvest. Even now the reaper draws his wages, even now he harvests the crop for eternal life, so that the sower and the reaper may be glad together. Thus the saying "One sows and another reaps" is true. I sent you to reap what you have not worked for. Others have done the hard work, and you have reaped the benefits of their labor. (Jn. 4:35–38)

Then he said to his disciples, "The harvest is plentiful but the workers are few." (Mt. 9:37)

A common pitfall in evangelism is doing the wrong thing at the wrong time. We plant the gospel but dig it up every day to inspect its growth without waiting for the harvest, or we sit around immobile when the harvest is ripe.

KINDNESS

But the fruit of the Spirit is love, joy, peace, patience, *kindness*, goodness, faithfulness. (Gal. 5:22)

Kindness is one of the greatest weapons in kingdom warfare. It is God's principal instrument for leading people to repentance.

> Or do you show contempt for the riches of His *kindness*, tolerance and patience, not realizing that *God's kindness leads you towards repentance?* (Rom. 2:4)

God used Paul to give Timothy instruction on how to witness and how not to witness:

> Don't have anything to do with foolish and stupid arguments, because you know they produce quarrels. And *the Lord's servant* must not quarrel; instead, he *must be kind to everyone*, able to teach, not resentful. Those who oppose him he must gently instruct, in the hope that God will grant them *repentance* leading them to a knowledge of the truth, and that they will come to their senses and escape from the trap of the devil, who has taken them captive to do his will. (2 Tim. 2:23–26)

People do not usually associate the words "kindness" and "repentance." Repent is considered a harsh word. But kindness and gentleness are God's means of bringing people to repentance.

> Love is patient, *love is kind*. It does not envy, it does not boast, it is not proud. (1 Cor. 13:4)

> We put no stumbling block in anyone's path, so that our ministry will not be discredited. Rather, as servants of God we commend ourselves in every way: in great endurance; in troubles, hardships and distresses; in beatings, imprisonments and riots; in hard work, sleepless nights and hunger; in purity, understanding, patience and *kindness*; in the Holy Spirit and in sincere love; in truthful speech and in the power

of God; with *weapons of righteousness in the right hand and in the left.* (2 Cor. 6:3–7)

If we are witnessing in power in the Holy Spirit (1 Thess. 1:5), we will be witnessing with kindness.

GOODNESS

But the fruit of the Spirit is love, joy, peace, patience, kindness, *goodness*, faithfulness. (Gal. 5:22)

He was a *good* man, full of the Holy Spirit and faith, and a great number of people were brought to the Lord. (Acts 11:24)

Barnabas was full of the Holy Spirit. He was also a good man. This is not surprising, since the fruit of the Spirit is goodness. Goodness is a characteristic of being filled with the Holy Spirit and a characteristic of effective preaching. In Acts 11, Barnabas preached, and a great number of people were brought to the Lord.

Preaching the content of the Good News without *being good* is contradictory.

Whoever claims to live in Him must walk as Jesus did. (1 Jn. 2:6)

If we are going to *talk* the good news, we must *walk* the good news. How we live our day-to-day lives is part of our witness for Christ. Our lives are a gospel, read by everyone who interacts with us.

FAITHFULNESS

> But the fruit of the Spirit is love, joy, peace, patience, kindness, goodness, *faithfulness*, gentleness and self-control. Against such things there is no law. (Gal. 5:22–23)

Faithfulness is God's nature which He has imparted to us.

> God, who has called you into fellowship with his Son Jesus Christ our Lord, is *faithful*. (1 Cor. 1:9)

> No temptation has seized you except what is common to man. And God is *faithful*; he will not let you be tempted beyond what you can bear. But when you are tempted, he will also provide a way out so that you can stand up under it. (1 Cor. 10:13)

> If we confess our sins, he is *faithful* and just and will forgive us our sins and purify us from all unrighteousness. (1 Jn. 1:9)

How do we apply God's faithfulness in evangelism?

> This, then, is how you ought to regard us: as servants of Christ and as those entrusted with the mysteries God has revealed. Now it is required that those who have been given a trust must prove *faithful*. (1 Cor. 4:1–2)

We have been entrusted with the ministry of the gospel and the message of the gospel. We apply God's faithfulness in evangelism by accepting the responsibility of the ministry and by not deviating from the message.

> *All this is from God, who reconciled us to himself through Christ and gave us the ministry of reconciliation: that God was reconciling the world to himself in Christ, not counting people's sins against them. And he has committed to us the message of*

reconciliation. We are therefore Christ's ambassadors, as though God were making his appeal through us. We implore you on Christ's behalf: Be reconciled to God. God made him who had no sin to be sin for us, so that in him we might become the righteousness of God. (2 Cor. 5:18–21)

GENTLENESS

But the fruit of the Spirit is love, joy, peace, patience, kindness, goodness, faithfulness, *gentleness* and self-control. Against such things there is no law. (Gal. 5:22–23)

But the wisdom that is from above is first pure, then peaceable, *gentle*, easy to be entreated, full of mercy and good fruits, without partiality, and without hypocrisy. (Jas. 3:17, KJV)

These two quotations are not surprising; gentleness is something we should expect from a loving God. However, the fruit and wisdom of gentleness are given to *us*, and God expects *us* to be gentle. Here are two examples:

Those who oppose him he must *gently* instruct, in the hope that God will grant them repentance leading them to a knowledge of the truth. (2 Tim. 2:25)

But in your hearts set apart Christ as Lord. Always be prepared to give an answer to everyone who asks you to give the reason for the hope that you have. But do this with *gentleness* and respect. (1 Pet. 3:15)

We are gentle with fragile things such as china figurines and with helpless things like newborn babies. We are not accustomed to being gentle towards enemies of the gospel and people who are belligerently anti-Christian. The fragile and the helpless engender a gentle response. We are afraid they will break if we are not gentle. This response is not a fruit of the Spirit. It is something the majority of people in this world have naturally. The antagonist does not evoke a gentle response, so we are not gentle with him. We do not care whether he is breakable.

When the servant of the Lord has the gentleness that is from above, he corrects his *opponents* gently. Like the other fruits of the Spirit, this gentleness is not something we can fabricate. It is given to us, and it is *commanded*.

God requires us to refute the opposition and yet not be quarrelsome. 2 Timothy 2:24–25 confirms this teaching: "and the Lord's servant must not quarrel; instead he must be kind to everyone, able to teach, not resentful. Those who oppose him, he must *gently* instruct."

There is increasing opposition today to Christians and to sound doctrine. Elders must be able to refute those in opposition (Titus 1:9), but they must do it *gently*, kindly, and without quarreling. We can *choose* to be gentle because we already have gentleness through the presence of the Holy Spirit.

SELF-CONTROL

> But the fruit of the Spirit is love, joy, peace, patience, kindness, goodness, faithfulness, gentleness and *self-control*. Against such things there is no law. (Gal. 5:22–23)

The book of Titus gives several reasons for exercising self-control:

> You must teach what is in accord with sound doctrine. Teach the older men to be temperate, worthy of respect, *self-controlled*, and sound in faith, in love and in endurance. Likewise, teach the older women to be reverent in the way they live, not to be slanderers or addicted to much wine, but to

teach what is good. Then they can train the younger women to love their husbands and children, to *be self-controlled* and pure, to be busy at home, to be kind, and to be subject to their husbands, *so that no one will malign the word of God.* Similarly, encourage the young men to be *self-controlled.* In everything set them an example by doing what is good. In your teaching show integrity, seriousness and soundness of speech that cannot be condemned, *so that those who oppose you may be ashamed because they have nothing bad to say about us.* (Tit. 2:1–8)

You may know of witnessing situations where the Christian did not exhibit self-control—perhaps he got loud or angry or annoyed, and his annoyance showed. To have power without love is awful. To have power without self-control is disastrous. Power keeps us from being timid or ashamed of Jesus Christ. Self-control keeps us from acting in ways of which we *should* be ashamed.

Most witnessing situations where self-control is lacking occur when a Christian is caught not knowing the answers. Consequently, he raises his voice to get false authority.

Self-control is part of the fruit of the Spirit. It is aided by confidence in the Lord and His Word and by preparation in knowledge of the Word. God has given us a spirit of power, love, and self-control to keep us from acting in shameful ways as we share the Good News.

For it is God's will that by doing good you should silence the ignorant talk of foolish men. (1 Pet. 2:15)

Wouldn't it be wonderful if foolish men were silent and no one maligned the word of God because they had nothing bad to say?

CHAPTER 9

HUMILITY

Humility is not just an admirable character trait. It is essential in the presentation of the gospel.

> Come to me, all you who are weary and burdened, and I will give you rest. Take my yoke upon you and learn from me, for I am gentle and *humble* in heart, and you will find rest for your souls. (Mt. 11:28–29)

The gentle imperative "Come to me" emphasizes an exceptional quality of Jesus: His humility and meekness. This is wonderfully described in Philippians 2:5–11:

> Your attitude should be the same as that of Christ Jesus: Who, being in very nature God, did not consider equality with God something to be grasped, but made himself nothing, taking the very nature of a servant, being made in human likeness. And being found in appearance as a man, he *humbled* himself and became obedient to death—even death on a cross! Therefore God exalted him to the highest place and gave him the name that is above every name, that at the name of Jesus every knee should bow, in heaven and on earth

and under the earth, and every tongue confess that Jesus Christ is Lord, to the glory of God the Father.

Jesus carried out a sequence of humble actions that resulted in our salvation:

1. He made himself nothing, taking the very nature of a servant, being made in human likeness.
2. Being found in appearance as a man, he *humbled* himself and became obedient to death . . . even death on a *cross.*

Therefore God exalted Him. Verse 5 tells us that our attitude should be the same as Christ Jesus. That means that when we proclaim the gospel of Christ, including how and why He came to die, we should be like Him in humility. The humility of the messenger should match the humility that established the message.

> To this you were called, because Christ suffered for you, leaving you *an example,* that you should follow in his steps. (1 Pet. 2:21)

> For everyone who exalts himself will be humbled, and he who *humbles himself* will be exalted. (Lk. 14:11)

> For whoever exalts himself will be *humbled*, and whoever *humbles* himself will be exalted. (Mt. 23:12)

> As a prisoner for the Lord, then, I urge you to live a life worthy of the calling you have received. Be *completely humble* and gentle; be patient, bearing with one another in love. (Eph. 4:1–2)

God exalts those who have humbled themselves. The exalting comes second. If we put self-exaltation first, humiliation is the result. If we exalt ourselves, we are arrogant. We do not look like Jesus to the unsaved.

Here is how Paul humbly identified with people. The reason for this humility was the salvation of as many as possible:

> Though I am free and belong to no man, I make myself a slave to everyone, to win as many as possible. To the Jews I became like a Jew, *to win the Jews*. To those under the law I became like one under the law (though I myself am not under the law), so as *to win those under the law*. To those not having the law I became like one not having the law (though I am not free from God's law but am under Christ's law), so as *to win those not having the law*. To the weak I became weak, to win the weak. I have become all things to all men so that by all possible means I might save some. (1 Corinthians 9:19–22)

CHAPTER 10

THE WORD

of God

The Scriptures are to be wielded. Ephesians 6:17 describes the word of God as an offensive weapon:

> Take the helmet of salvation and the *sword of the Spirit*, which is the *word of God*.

Again in Hebrews 4:12:

> For the *word of God* is living and active. Sharper than any *double-edged sword*, it penetrates even to dividing soul and spirit, joints and marrow; it judges the thoughts and attitudes of the heart.

Second Timothy 4:2 commands us to use the sword of the Spirit:

> *Preach the word*; be prepared in season and out of season; correct, rebuke and encourage—with great patience and careful instruction.

Preaching Christ causes faith. But we are to preach Christ as He is presented to us in the Scriptures:

> How, then, can they call on the one they *have not believed in?* And how can they believe in the one of whom they *have not heard?* And how can they hear without someone *preaching* to them? And how can they preach unless they are sent? As it is written, "How beautiful are the feet of those who bring good news!" But not all the Israelites accepted the good news. For Isaiah says, "Lord, who has believed our message?" Consequently, *faith comes from hearing the message, and the message is heard through the word of Christ.* (Rom. 10:14–17)

> No one can come to me unless the *Father who sent Me draws him*, and I will raise him up at the last day. It is written in the Prophets: "They will all be taught by God." *Everyone who listens to the Father and learns from Him comes to Me.* (Jn. 6:44–45)

> Therefore, since the promise of entering His rest still stands, let us be careful that none of you be found to have fallen short of it. For we also have had the gospel *preached to us, just as they did*; but the message they heard was of no value to them, because *those who heard did not combine it with faith.* Now we who have believed enter that rest, just as God has said, "So I declared an oath in My anger, 'They shall never enter My rest.'" (Heb. 4:1–3)

It is the gospel that causes belief. Some people hear the gospel but refuse to learn, refuse to combine their hearing with faith, refuse to repent. However, the majority of the lost have a different problem. They cannot believe because they have not yet heard the gospel.

CHAPTER 11

THE BAPTISM

of the Spirit

Whenever we use the weapons of the Holy Spirit (preaching, prayer, gifts, and the fruit of the Spirit), the Spirit works in the lives of sinners.

> Jesus answered, "I tell you the truth, no one can enter the kingdom of God unless he is born of water and the Spirit. Flesh gives birth to flesh, but *the Spirit gives birth to spirit.* You should not be surprised at my saying, *'You must be born again.'*" (Jn. 3:5–7)

> Then Peter said to them, "Repent, and let every one of you be baptized in the name of Jesus Christ for the remission of sins; and you shall *receive the gift of the Holy Spirit.* (Acts 2:38)

> Then I remembered what the Lord had said: "John baptized with water, but you will be *baptized with the Holy Spirit."* (Acts 11:16)

> For we were all *baptized by one Spirit* into one body—whether Jews or Greeks, slave or free—and we were all given the one Spirit to drink. (1 Cor. 12:13)

When they arrived, they prayed for them that they might receive the Holy Spirit, because the *Holy Spirit had not yet come upon any of them*; they had simply been baptized into the name of the Lord Jesus. (Acts 8:15–16)

CHAPTER 12

TERROR

Fear is not necessarily a bad motivation. In certain circumstances, it is an entirely reasonable response.

> Men will faint from *terror*, apprehensive of what is coming on the world, for the heavenly bodies will be shaken. At that time they will see the Son of Man coming in a cloud with power and great glory. (Lk. 21:26–27)

> *Terror* and pit and snare await you, people of the earth. (Is. 24:17)

Recently I was talking with a twelve-year-old boy who was very rebellious towards his father. As I taught him the Good News, he interrupted to tell me his greatest motivation to become a Christian was fear of being cast into the lake of fire. He apparently received Christ, for his mother told me he has become a very different boy.

Terror is abject fear. There has always been terror in war. The main object of terrorism is *not* killing innocent people.

The purpose of terrorism is to cause fear in the *survivors*, a fear that immobilizes them.

During World War II, more people were killed in Tokyo and Yokohama by incendiary bombs than were killed by the atomic bombs dropped on Hiroshima and Nagasaki. It was the *terror* caused by the latter which brought about Japan's surrender.

Terror *anticipates* certain destruction. It is a message to those who are still living. It is a message of extreme fear based upon reality, not imagination. Jesus taught terror (Mt. 13:40–42, 49–50). Isaiah taught terror (Is. 24:17). Jeremiah taught terror (Jer. 7:20). The apostle John taught terror (Rev. 6:15–17).

Jesus used terror to help people believe in Himself:

> For God so loved the world that He gave His one and only Son, that whoever believes in Him shall not perish but have eternal life. For God did not send His Son into the world to condemn the world, but to save the world through Him. Whoever believes in Him is not condemned, but *whoever does not believe stands condemned already* because he has not believed in the name of God's one and only Son. (Jn. 3:16–18)

> Whoever believes in the Son has eternal life, but whoever rejects the Son will not see life, for *God's wrath remains on him*. (Jn. 3:36)

Notice the phrases, "shall not perish," "condemned already," and "God's wrath remains on him." These are not empty threats.

In 2 Corinthians 5:9–11, the Apostle Paul told us to use fear to persuade men. This fear comes from what takes place at the judgment seat of Christ.

Wherefore we labor, that, whether present or absent, we may be accepted of him. For we must all appear before the judgment seat of Christ; that every one may receive the things done in his body, according to that he hath done, whether it be good or bad. Knowing therefore *the terror of the Lord*, we *persuade men*; but we are made manifest unto God; and I trust also are made manifest in your consciences. (2 Cor. 5:9–11)

Then I saw a great white throne and Him who was seated on it. Earth and sky fled from his presence, and there was no place for them. And I saw the dead, great and small, standing before the throne, and books were opened. Another book was opened, which is the book of life. The dead were judged according to what they had done as recorded in the books. The sea gave up the dead that were in it, and death and Hades gave up the dead that were in them, and each person was judged according to what he had done. Then death and Hades were thrown into the lake of fire. The lake of fire is the second death. If anyone's name was not found written in the book of life, he was *thrown into the lake of fire*. (Rev. 20:11–15)

This is a story I heard over fifty years ago: There was once a famous Anglican missionary who had a reputation for being a hell-fire preacher. He was very effective in describing judgment. Upon his return to England from missionary work, his bishop assigned him to preach in a village church. When he heard who was coming to preach, the vicar of the church became very anxious for his flock. He was concerned what the missionary would preach and what the effect would be on his congregation.

The vicar met the missionary at the train. After some small talk, the vicar asked him what his text would be on Sunday. The missionary replied he had not yet decided, and did the pastor have any suggestions? The pastor replied, "We here in civilized England are not big on judgment. Any message on the love of God would be fine." The missionary answered, "Wonderful. How about John 3:16, 'For God so loved the world'?" The pastor, relieved, said "That will be just fine."

On Sunday morning in the village church, the missionary opened his Bible to John 3 and began to read. "For God so loved the world that He gave His only begotten Son, that whosoever believeth in Him should not . . ." He stopped and started over. "For God so loved the world that He gave His only begotten Son, that whosoever believeth in Him should not . . ." He stopped again, turned to the vicar and said, "What shall I do now, vicar?"

The love of God is the salvation from death and from the fear of death. The only reason God expressed His love to man in the death of His Son was that man was under judgment because of his sin. *Judgment must be preached first, or the love of God makes no sense.*

> Since the children have flesh and blood, He too shared in their humanity so that by His death He might destroy Him who holds the power of death—that is, the devil—and free those who all their lives were held in slavery by their *fear of death.* (Heb. 2:14–15)

> This is how God showed His love among us: He sent His one and only Son into the world that we might live through Him. This is love: not that we loved God, but that He loved us and sent His Son as an atoning sacrifice for our sins. (1 Jn. 4:9–10)

People surrender or flee when they are terrified. Terror is an effective weapon.

It is a dreadful thing to fall into the hands of the living God. (Heb. 10:31)

There are far, far too many people going to hell *unafraid* because they have not been scared. People must be informed of the sure judgment of God. If they are afraid, they might be open to the salvation available in the love of God for sinners.

There is no fear in love. But perfect love drives out fear, because fear has to do with punishment. The one who fears is not made perfect in love. (1 Jn. 4:18)

FEAR

Consider using the following truths with unbelievers.

I tell you, my friends, do not be afraid of those who kill the body and after that can do no more. But I will show you whom you should fear: Fear Him who, after the killing of the body, has power to throw you into hell. Yes, I tell you, fear Him. (Lk. 12:4–5)

We are given a choice of whom to fear. We can fear those who can kill the body, or we can fear Him who sentences people to the second death (Lk. 12:4–5).

He who was seated on the throne said, "I am making everything new!" Then He said, "Write this down, for *these words are trustworthy and true.*" He said to me, "It is done. I am the Alpha and the Omega, the Beginning and the End. To him who is thirsty I will give to drink without cost from the spring of the water of life. He who overcomes will inherit all this, and I will be his God and he will be My son. But the cowardly, the unbelieving, the vile, the murderers, the sexually immoral, those who practice magic arts, the idolaters and all liars—*their place will be in the fiery lake of burning sulfur. This is the second death.*" (Rev. 21:5–8)

The voice is from the great white throne at the end of history. The voice said, "Write this down, for these words are trustworthy and true." If we fear God, He delivers us from both the fear of the first and of the second death.

We can flee Satan, but no one can successfully flee from God, nor can we fight with Him and win.

> Where can I go from your Spirit? Where can I flee from your presence? If I go up to the heavens, you are there; if I make my bed in the depths, you are there. If I rise on the wings of the dawn, if I settle on the far side of the sea, even there your hand will guide me, your right hand will hold me fast. If I say, "Surely the darkness will hide me and the light become night around me," even the darkness will not be dark to you; the night will shine like the day, for darkness is as light to you. (Ps. 139:7–12)

Are we willing and ready to preach the judgment seat of Christ? Jesus did it. Paul did it. John and Peter did it. If we leave out the bad news, people have no reason to embrace the Good News.

CHAPTER 13

OUR OWN

Testimony

We are not just messengers in our presentation of the gospel. We are also to serve as *witnesses*.

> They overcame him by the blood of the Lamb and by the *word of their testimony*; they did not love their lives so much as to shrink from death. (Rev. 12:11)

The story of Paul's conversion is told three different times in the book of Acts. It is first recounted in chapter nine. Later Paul retells the story to the lynch mob in Jerusalem in front of the Roman barracks in Acts 22. The third time was two years later, in Acts 26. Paul spent those years in prison in Caesarea. He gave his testimony to the governor Festus, and to King Agrippa and his sister Bernice in an audience room with high-ranking officials and the leading men of the city.

I encourage you to write out your own testimony. Use this testimony to give the saving message to people whose eyes are already open and who are hungry for the light of the gospel. Tell what you were like before, when you first became interested in Christianity, how you heard or read the gospel, when you made a decision, and the results. Then send it to someone who is not a Christian and tell it to people often.

CHAPTER 14

APOLOGIA,

Apologetics, and Reasoning

APOLOGIA

Apologia: a defense, especially of one's opinions, position, or actions.[1]

Apologia: to give an account (legal plea) of oneself.[2]

The Greek word *apologia* appears ten times in the New Testament. In the KJV it is always translated "answer" or "answered." In the NIV it is translated "defend" nine times and "answer" once. Here are eight of the ten occurrences:

> When you are brought before synagogues, rulers and authorities, do not worry about how you will *defend* yourselves or what you will say, for the Holy Spirit will teach you at that time what you should say. (Lk. 12:11–12)

1. *Webster's Ninth New Collegiate Dictionary* (Merriam-Webster, 1991).
2. *Strong's Exhaustive Concordance of the Bible* (Thomas Nelson Publishers, 1984).

But before all this, they will seize you and persecute you. They will hand you over to synagogues and put you in prison, and you will be brought before kings and governors, and all on account of my name. And so you will bear testimony to me. But make up your mind not to worry beforehand how you will *defend* yourselves. For I will give you words and wisdom that none of your adversaries will be able to resist or contradict. (Lk. 21:12–15)

When the governor motioned for him to speak, Paul replied: "I know that for a number of years you have been a judge over this nation; so I gladly make my *defense*." (Acts 24:10)

Then Paul made his *defense*: "I have done nothing wrong against the Jewish law or against the temple or against Caesar." (Acts 25:8)

Then Agrippa said to Paul, "You have permission to speak for yourself." So Paul motioned with his hand and began his *defense*. (Acts 26:1–2)

This is my *defense* to those who sit in judgment on me. (1 Cor. 9:3)

At my first *defense*, no one came to my support, but everyone deserted me. May it not be held against them. But the Lord stood at my side and gave me strength, so that through me the message might be fully proclaimed and all the Gentiles might hear it. And I was delivered from the lion's mouth. (2 Tim. 4:16–17)

But in your hearts revere Christ as Lord. Always be prepared to give an *answer* to everyone who asks you to give the reason for the hope that you have. But do this with gentleness and respect, keeping a clear conscience, so that those who speak maliciously against your good behavior in Christ may be ashamed of their slander. (1 Pet. 3:15–16)

In the first two quotations, Jesus tells us not to plan beforehand when we are brought before judges. The next three are the witnessing and preaching opportunities Paul took before Felix, Agrippa, and Caesar. His defense to the Christians (1 Corinthians 9) is mostly about preaching the gospel. The last passage tells us how to answer questions with the *gospel.*

The way *apologia* is used in the Scriptures has very little resemblance to apologetics today. Paul's defense was an aggressive *offense with the gospel* to his listeners.

APOLOGETICS

Apologetics (singular): The branch of theology that deals with the defense of a religious faith on the basis of reason.[3]

Apologetics has crept into the church as a weapon for evangelism. Today there are many books available on Christian apologetics. At best, apologetics can be useful pre-evangelism. Several things make it difficult to use as a tool *in* evangelism:

1. It is defensive.

2. It is based on reason.

3. It does not create faith.

4. The gospel is not normally included in it.

5. The average person does not understand the presuppositions or the reasoning used.

6. Jesus and the apostles did not use it the way it is used today.

---

3. *The World Book Encyclopedia Dictionary,* ed. Clarence L. Barnhart (Chicago: Thorndike-Barnhart, 1963).

7. When used in discussion, it tends to turn the conversation into a debate/argument, and Christians are not to argue like that.
8. It is not declarative. It does not proclaim or preach.
9. It does not deal with sin.
10. It defends the use of the Word of God *as* an authority rather than using the Word of God *with* authority.

I have no objection to books on apologetics when used as eye-openers for the unbeliever. However, there are much better eye-openers. Apologetic books are much more helpful to Christians who feel vulnerable under attack when they are accused of being irrational (although, even there, apologetics does not necessarily increase faith in the believer).

The following is an example of *not* using apologetics. In the fall of 1954, I was on the staff of Commander Naval Forces, Far East in Yokosuka, Japan. While there, I got to know a young naval officer whose favorite word for others was "stupid." One day he heard me say something positive about my boss whom he had already tagged as stupid. Of course, that made me stupid, too. Sometime later, the two of us were having a professional conversation in the Bachelor Officers' Quarters. Over the course of the conversation, he came to realize that I knew more than he did about the subject, both from my years of experience and from graduate school. I realized that I had gotten out of his "stupid" book. At the end of the conversation, as I was going to my room, I turned around and said, "Vic, the next time I talk to you, I will talk to you about God."

Two days later I took my Bible and went up to his room. He was looking in the mirror and tying his tie. I said, "I came to talk to you about God. Unless you have other plans, I will stay."

He replied, "I had other plans, but I just changed them. Sit down."

I sat down. Vic went to his closet and pulled out a book. He sat on the bunk and opened to a page about two-thirds of the way through the book. I could see a paragraph underlined in red on the page. Vic Jensen was an atheist with a degree in philosophy from a Jesuit university. He said, "Shoot. Prove to me there is a God."

"Vic," I told him, "I did not come to prove God. I came to declare Him."

"If you do not prove God, there is no basis for conversation."

"Suppose there is a God," I said. "He made billions of stars, billions of rain drops, billions of buttercups, and billions of people. You stand up to Him and say, 'Show me, and I will believe.' He doesn't have to show you—you are one billionth! I am His representative. I do not have to show you, and I will not show you."

He closed his book. "What is the subject, then?"

"I thought I would start with sin."

"Sin? There is no such thing as sin! Whose sin?"

"Since you asked, it is the sin in Vic Jensen."

"There is no sin in me!"

"Do you mean to say that you have no conscience?"

He changed the subject. "What are you going to use for an authority?"

"I brought my Bible. I thought I would use that for an authority."

"You can't use that," he said.

"Why?"

"For two reasons. First, the Bible is not allowed in intercollegiate debate, and second, I do not accept it as an authority."

"First, this is not intercollegiate debate. It is war, and the rules are different. Second, I do not care that you do not accept it as an authority. Suppose I have a two-edged sword in my hand, and I say to you, 'Jensen, I'm going to chop off your head.' You laugh and say, 'You can't chop off my head because I don't believe that's a sword.' Then it's my turn to laugh. 'I will have your head.' If I sheath the sword because you don't believe it is a sword, that does not prove it isn't a sword; it only proves that *I* don't believe it's a sword. 'The Word of God is quick and powerful and sharper than any two-edged sword, dividing asunder between the soul and spirit, joints and marrow, discerning the thoughts and intents of the heart.'[4] I'm going to have your head."

I continued, "What do you think the Bible is? Fiction?"

"Yeah, fiction."

"You mean like *Pogo* or *Terry and the Pirates* in the funny papers?"

"About in that category."

"Do you read *Pogo*?"

"Oh, yeah, I love *Pogo*."

"*Terry and the Pirates*?"

"Yeah, I read fiction all the time."

I said, "Then you won't mind if I read you a few chapters of fiction."

Why do people not want you to read the Word of God to them? Because they do *not* believe in it? No: because they are afraid it might be true. I said, "If it's fiction, you won't mind at all," and I read him the first eight chapters of Romans. He sat and listened—no quarrels, no arguments. A few days later he came down to my room and said, "Let's have some more of the book." I read him the first five chapters of Acts.

4. Hebrews 4:12

That time I gave him a Bible so he could follow along as I read out loud. Later I read him the next thirteen chapters of Acts, the resurrection account in the four gospels, and 1 Corinthians 15.

REASONING

There is a reasoning which is effective in evangelism. It is not apologetic in character. It is not defensive. In fact, it is an aggressive *offense.* It is the kind of biblical reasoning used in Peter's preaching in Acts 2, Stephen's preaching in Acts 7, and Paul's preaching in Acts 17, and the preaching of the apostles in Corinth (1 Cor. 1–2).

These two books are examples of this kind of reasoning today:

- *Mere Christianity* by C.S. Lewis. This book is extra-biblical and starts with the subject of sin.
- *Basic Christianity* by J.R.W. Stott. This book reasons within a biblical framework starting with the deity of Jesus Christ.

CHAPTER 15

NOT OUR WEAPONS

Scripture teaches us the weapons we are to use. But there is another important category for us to learn—what kind of weapons are off limits to us.

> For the appeal we make does not spring from error or impure motives, nor are we trying to trick you. On the contrary, we speak as men approved by God to be entrusted with the gospel. We are not trying to please men but God, who tests our hearts. You know we never used flattery, nor did we put on a mask to cover up greed—God is our witness. We were not looking for praise from men, not from you or anyone else. (1 Thess. 2:3–6)

Notice the things that the apostles refused to use in reaching people:

1. error
2. impure motives
3. trickery
4. pleasing men

5. flattery

6. masks to cover up greed

Unfortunately, all of these are used by some Christians who claim to be doing evangelism. Avoid them! From saying that you "see that hand" when you don't (#3) to telling someone that they would make a fine Christian (#5), we have not obeyed the Scripture carefully at this point.

Here are two more things to be avoided in evangelism:

- Human wisdom: *For Christ did not send me to baptize, but to preach the gospel—not with words of human wisdom, lest the cross of Christ be emptied of its power (1 Cor. 1:17).*

- Foolish and stupid arguments and quarrels: *Don't have anything to do with foolish and stupid arguments, because you know they produce quarrels (2 Tim. 2:23).*

PART 2

TACTICS

As was stated earlier, the principles of war were covered in my first book on evangelism. But the principles have to be remembered at the points of application. This section presupposes that you have already read and understand *Principles of War*.

CHAPTER I

THE OBJECTIVE

An army needs to understand in what direction it is supposed to march.

Then Jesus came to them and said, "All authority in heaven and on earth has been given to Me. Therefore go and *make disciples of all nations*, baptizing them in the name of the Father and of the Son and of the Holy Spirit, and *teaching them to obey* everything I have commanded you. And surely I am with you always, to the very end of the age." (Mt. 28:18–20)

Jesus' first statement in the Great Commission is indicative: "All authority in heaven and earth has been given to Me." That authority is absolute and comprehensive. This results in an imperative: "Make disciples!"

He told them, "This is what is written: The Christ will suffer and rise from the dead on the third day, and repentance and forgiveness of sins will be preached in His name to all nations, beginning at Jerusalem. You are witnesses of these

things. I am going to send you what My Father has promised; but stay in the city until you have been clothed with
power from on high." (Lk. 24:46–49)

This is the means of making disciples. Jesus Christ's work
was to suffer for sins and rise from the dead. The disciples'
work was to preach with the authority of His name. They
were to preach repentance and forgiveness of sins to all nations, starting in Jerusalem, and they were to preach it with
power from on high:

> But you will receive power when the Holy Spirit comes on
> you; and you will be My witnesses in *Jerusalem*, and in all
> *Judea* and *Samaria*, and to *the ends of the earth* (Acts 1:8)

Jesus' operational order is clear: 1) The apostles are to make
disciples, 2) beginning in *Jerusalem*, 3) via *adjacent countries,*
4) to the *ends of the earth, all nations.*

> When He saw the crowds, He had compassion on them, be-
> cause they were harassed and helpless, like sheep without
> a shepherd. Then He said to His disciples, "The harvest is
> plentiful but the workers are few. Ask the Lord of the har-
> vest, therefore, to send out workers into His harvest field."
> (Mt. 9:36–38)

Christ commands the apostles to pray for more harvesters.
If it is still true that the harvest is plentiful and the laborers
are few, then this prayer is still necessary today. If it is still
true, then there are more non-Christians ready to become
Christians than there are Christians who are ready to help
them believe and repent. To be blunt, there are more people
who want to get into the Kingdom than there are Christians
who want them in.

I will rescue you from your own people and from the Gentiles. I am sending you to them to *open their eyes* and *turn them from darkness to light*, and *from the power of Satan to God*, so that they may receive forgiveness of sins and a place among those who are sanctified by faith in me. (Acts 26:17–18)

This is the great commission given by the Lord Jesus to Saul of Tarsus, making him an apostle, a "sent one," and this happened the instant he became a believer. This is the One who has been given all authority in heaven and earth giving instructions on evangelism to one of His greatest followers. Let us look at those instructions:

1. Open their eyes.
2. Turn them from darkness to light.
3. Turn them from the power of Satan to God.

Paul had to do those three things in order to get two things for the people he witnessed to:

1. Forgiveness of sins
2. A place among those who are sanctified by faith in Him

This is the essence of the battle plan assigned to man for the conquest of the world.

Here is the command stated again:

Then Jesus came to them and said, "All authority in heaven and on earth has been given to me. Therefore go and make disciples of all nations, baptizing them in the name of the Father and of the Son and of the Holy Spirit, *and teaching them to obey everything I have commanded you.* And surely I am with you always, to the very end of the age." (Mt. 28:18–20)

All new Christians are to be taught to obey everything Jesus commanded, including this command. This means that the Great Commission is self-perpetuating. Each generation of Christians is supposed to hand it off to the next generation.

> On that day a great persecution broke out against the church at Jerusalem, and *all except the apostles* were scattered throughout Judea and Samaria . . . Those who had been scattered *preached the word wherever they went.* (Acts 8:1b, 4)

In the first century, thousands of Christians left Jerusalem, preaching the gospel everywhere they went. But the apostles (the official "evangelists") stayed in Jerusalem.

We would be concerned if we knew that there were active terrorists in every neighborhood. What we don't realize is that the Enemy *has* such spiritual terrorists everywhere. Is the *world* concerned that we have *active effective* evangelists in *every neighborhood*? If we did have them, believe me, the Enemy would take every means to silence them. We do have them, but they are not being effective. It seems that our sleeper cells went to sleep.

> I have appeared to you to appoint you as a servant and as a witness of what you have seen of me and what I will show you. (Acts 26:16)

> Go! This man is a chosen instrument to carry my name before the Gentiles and their kings and before the people of Israel. (Acts 9:15)

> At once he began to preach in the synagogues that Jesus is the son of God. (Acts 9:20)

The common element in these three verses is that the Apostle Paul was sent as an evangelist at the time of his conversion. His position as an evangelist is one of the reasons the Bible gives for his conversion, and upon being converted he became that evangelist without further training or growth in the Lord. We might conclude that Paul was unique in this and that the rest of us cannot, nor are we expected to, follow this pattern. Or we can say this is God's requirement for us *all*. The apostle says exactly that in his second letter to Corinth:

> And he died for all, that *those who live* should no longer live for themselves but for him who died for them and was raised again. So from now on we regard no one from a worldly point of view. Though we once regarded Christ in this way, we do so no longer. Therefore, *if anyone is in Christ*, he is a new creation; the old has gone, the new has come! All this is from God, who reconciled us to himself *through Christ and gave us the ministry of reconciliation:* that God was reconciling the world to himself in Christ, not counting men's sins against them. And he has committed to us the *message of reconciliation.* We are therefore Christ's ambassadors, as though God were making his appeal through us. We implore you on Christ's behalf: Be reconciled to God. God made him who had no sin to be sin for us, so that in him we might become the righteousness of God. (2 Cor. 5:15–21)

When Paul speaks in verse 15 of "those who live," and in verse 17 of, "anyone in Christ," he is clearly not speaking of himself alone, but of all believers. He goes on to say this: "who reconciled us to himself through Christ, and gave us the *ministry* of reconciliation." The "us" is "anyone in Christ." Therefore, anyone who is in Christ, as soon as he is in Christ, is immediately commissioned in the ministry of reconciliation at his conversion. The ministry of reconciliation is not only given to reconciled men: it is given at the moment of reconciliation. The demon-possessed man Jesus healed is an example of this:

As Jesus was getting into the boat, the man who had been demon-possessed begged to go with him. Jesus did not let him, but said, "Go home to your own people and tell them how much the Lord has done for you, and how he has had mercy on you." So the man went away and began to tell in the Decapolis how much Jesus had done for him. And all the people were amazed. (Mk. 5:18–20)

God has given us the *ministry* and the *message*. We are to preach the Word everywhere, just like the new Christians in Acts.

DECISIVE POINTS

A decisive point is a place where, if a battle were fought and won there, it would be a decisive victory, one that influences the whole war.

In the war for souls, the battles must be fought in every location on earth because our Lord Jesus Christ sent us *everywhere*.

Therefore go and make disciples of *all nations*, baptizing them in the name of the Father and of the Son and of the Holy Spirit. (Mt. 28:19)

He told them, "This is what is written: The Christ will suffer and rise from the dead on the third day, and repentance and forgiveness of sins will be preached in his name to *all nations*, beginning at Jerusalem." (Lk. 24:46–47)

But you will receive power when the Holy Spirit comes on you; and you will be my witnesses in Jerusalem, and in all Judea and Samaria, and to the *ends of the earth*. (Acts 1:8)

However, some places in particular are decisive points, and taking them will get the message to all places faster. If we want to reach the whole, then we should know what sort of places to concentrate on. Two questions determine whether a point is decisive: 1) Is it important? 2) Is it feasible?

Here are two biblical examples. First, in Ephesus:

> Paul entered the synagogue and spoke boldly there for three months, arguing persuasively about the kingdom of God. But some of them became obstinate; they refused to believe and publicly maligned the Way. So Paul left them. He took the disciples with him and had discussions daily in the lecture hall of Tyrannus. This went on for two years, so that *all the Jews and Greeks who lived in the province of Asia* heard the word of the Lord. (Acts 19:8–10)

In Thessalonica:

> You became imitators of us and of the Lord; in spite of severe suffering, you welcomed the message with the joy given by the Holy Spirit. *And so you became a model to all the believers in Macedonia and Achaia. The Lord's message rang out from you not only in Macedonia and Achaia—your faith in God has become known everywhere.* Therefore we do not need to say anything about it, for they themselves report what kind of reception you gave us. They tell how you turned to God from idols to serve the living and true God, and to wait for his Son from heaven, whom he raised from the dead—Jesus, who rescues us from the coming wrath. (1 Thess. 1:6–10)

These two cities were important and feasible, and they were therefore *decisive* in the effect they had on Asia, Macedonia, and Achaia.

Many years ago when praying about where to minister, I knew I wanted to go to a decisive point. There was no question in my mind that taking New York City would be decisive. If it could be taken it would mean that Wall Street, Madison Avenue, Broadway, NBC, ABC, CBS, Fox News, and ten million people would be saved. It would shake the world. It would be the greatest revival in history. However, I did not have the resources to bring the principles of war to bear on this stronghold of Satan. In other words, New York City could have been decisive, but it was not feasible. Without feasibility, a point is not decisive.

The Lord led me to small towns with major universities. The university makes such a place important. The small town makes it feasible. These are decisive points in any given state. Every student generation moves throughout the state and even the country upon graduation, and they can carry the message of Christ with them as they go. As in Ephesus, the battle can be fought in one place and win the whole state.

CHAPTER 2

ON THE OFFENSIVE

PREACH & PROCLAIM

Jesus said that the gates of Hades would not prevail against the Church. But city gates are not an offensive weapon. They are defensive, which means that the Church should be besieging them—and not the other way around.

> He told them, "This is what is written: The Christ will suffer and rise from the dead on the third day, and repentance and forgiveness of sins will be *preached* in His name to all nations, beginning at Jerusalem." (Lk. 24:46–47)

> As you go, *preach* this message: "The kingdom of heaven is near." (Mt. 10:7)

> The Spirit of the Lord is on me, and He has anointed me to *preach* good news to the poor. He has sent me to proclaim freedom for the prisoners and recovery of sight for the blind, to release the oppressed. (Lk. 4:18)

> In those days John the Baptist came, *preaching* in the Desert of Judea. (Mt. 3:1)

From that time on Jesus began to *preach*, "Repent, for the kingdom of heaven is near." (Mt. 4:17)

And how can they *preach* unless they are sent? As it is written, "How beautiful are the feet of those who bring good news!" (Rom. 10:15)

It has always been my ambition to *preach* the gospel where Christ was not known, so that I would not be building on someone else's foundation. (Rom. 15:20)

For Christ did not send me to baptize, but to *preach* the gospel—not with words of human wisdom, lest the cross of Christ be emptied of its power. (1 Cor. 1:17)

But we *preach* Christ crucified: a stumbling block to Jews and foolishness to Gentiles. (1 Cor. 1:23)

Yet when I *preach* the gospel, I cannot boast, for I am compelled to preach. Woe to me if I do not preach the gospel! (1 Cor. 9:16)

Preach the Word; be prepared in season and out of season; correct, rebuke and encourage—with great patience and careful instruction. (2 Tim. 4:2)

To preach is to declare, to speak with authority. It is one-way, dogmatic communication. It is not a discussion or a debate. It is a proclamation.

Therefore I glory in Christ Jesus in my service to God. I will not venture to speak of anything except what Christ has accomplished through me in leading the Gentiles to obey God by what I have said and done—by the power of signs and miracles, through the power of the Spirit. So from Jerusalem all the way around to Illyricum, I have fully *proclaimed* the gospel of Christ. (Rom. 15:17–19)

Once you were alienated from God and were enemies in your minds because of your evil behavior. But now He has reconciled you by Christ's physical body through death to present you holy in His sight, without blemish and free from accusation—if you continue in your faith, established and firm, not moved from the hope held out in the gospel. This is the gospel that you heard and that has been *proclaimed* to every creature under heaven, and of which I, Paul, have become a servant. (Col. 1:21–23)

But the Lord stood at my side and gave me strength, so that through me the message might be fully *proclaimed* and all the Gentiles might hear it. And I was delivered from the lion's mouth. (2 Tim. 4:17)

According to these verses, preaching and proclaiming is the way to spread the gospel. People do not think of this kind of presentation as loving, but it needs to actually *be* loving. You may have heard the expression "Don't preach to me." It is said with an emphasis that makes "preaching" sound like unkind, condemning speech. We have come to believe that preaching is unloving, and we do not want to be considered unloving, so we are either quiet or we soften our speech so it does not sound like preaching. This softening often leaves out parts of the gospel.

I remember once when an evangelist came to see me in the 1960s. He wanted to explain to me a new concept in communicating the gospel. It was called "sharing." This concept has since spread like wildfire. "Sharing" was meant to be inoffensive, more "loving," more "tactful."

The difficulty is that "sharing" has taken the place of preaching. We have bought the lie that because people take offense from preaching, the preaching must therefore not be loving. This is not true.

Here is a portion of Paul's first letter to the Thessalonians:

> We were not looking for praise from men, not from you or anyone else. As apostles of Christ we could have been a burden to you, but we were *gentle* among you, like a mother caring for her little children. *We loved you so much* that we were delighted to *share* with you not only the gospel of God *but our lives as well*, because you had become so dear to us. Surely you remember, brothers, our toil and hardship; we worked night and day in order not to be a burden to anyone while *we preached the gospel of God to you.* (1 Thess. 2:6–9)`

In this verse, "share" is good because it includes "our lives as well."

> For you know that we dealt with each of you as a father deals with his own children, *encouraging, comforting* and urging you to live lives worthy of God, who calls you into his kingdom and glory. (1 Thess. 2:11–12)

> Instead, speaking the *truth in love*, we will in all things grow up into him who is the Head, that is, Christ. (Eph. 4:15)

Paul loved *and* preached. It is not preaching (i.e. the method) that gives the right kind of offense; it is the content of the gospel message:

> Brothers, if I am still preaching circumcision, why am I still being persecuted? In that case *the offense of the cross* has been abolished. (Gal. 5:11)

It is the *cross* that gives offense. It is easy to leave out the cross in "sharing." The more we leave out, the easier it is to talk. It may be easy to talk to an unbeliever about "Jesus," but is harder to talk about the "Lord Jesus Christ." It is still harder to talk about sin. It is even harder to talk about 1)

Hell, 2) the cross, 3) the resurrection of Christ, and 4) repentance.

> It was he who gave some to be apostles, some to be prophets, some to be evangelists, and some to be pastors and teachers, *to prepare God's people for works of service, so that the body of Christ may be built up* until we all reach unity in the faith and in the knowledge of the Son of God and become mature, attaining to the whole measure of the fullness of Christ. (Eph. 4:11–13)

Pastors, teachers and evangelists are to teach the people to do works of service. They are not to do all of it themselves. We can divide the Christians into two groups:

1. Those whose vocation is preaching, teaching, and other works of service.
2. Those whose vocation is farming, business, laboring, housekeeping, or professional (attorneys, educators, physicians, etc.).

Most of the people in the first group (the ones who are trained) interact primarily with other Christians. They do not have much contact with unbelievers. They have to force themselves into contact with the rest of the world.

Most of the second group has normal, daily contact with unbelievers, but they very rarely preach the gospel because they are not taught how. Those in the first group are to *teach* those in the second group. The best means of teaching is example. The best way of learning is by imitating.

PREACH AS YOU GO

We shouldn't just preach when we get there—we should preach on the way.

As you go, *preach* this message: "The kingdom of heaven is near." (Mt. 10:7)

We often think of preaching as something that takes place at a certain location, at a certain hour, not too often, and not for too long. It also requires considerable preparation on the part of the preacher. However, this is not the kind of preaching Jesus was talking about when He gave His disciples the Great Commission in Matthew 28:19: *"As you go,* make disciples of all nations." Preaching and making disciples should be a normal part of our daily life, not a special part. Nor should it be only for pastors and full-time evangelists.

On that day a great persecution broke out against the church at Jerusalem, and *all except the apostles* were scattered throughout Judea and Samaria . . . Those who had been scattered *preached* the word wherever they went. (Acts 8:1,4)

Everyone *except* the apostles preached as they went. This was thousands of people, perhaps tens of thousands.

Christians are often intimidated by people who say, "Don't preach to me." Who made *them* the authority on what we should do? We are also intimidated by those who tell the laity that they are not "qualified" to preach. Obviously, the thousands who scattered from Jerusalem were qualified, and they were certainly not all ordained ministers.

The One who has all authority told us to preach as we go. Let us encourage one another to do this. When done with the weapon of the fullness of the Holy Spirit, this preaching is effective in the winning of souls.

CONCENTRATION

Concentration is outnumbering the opposition. The smallest ratio of effective concentration is two to one; but even being outnumbered five to two by the opposition is much better than being outnumbered five to one. Jesus practiced this in Scripture. He did not go alone until the cross. He picked twelve. Then He picked three at the transfiguration and in the garden. Jesus sent the seventy out *in pairs*:

> After this the Lord appointed seventy others and sent them two by two ahead of him to every town and place where he was about to go. (Lk. 10:1)

Paul and Barnabas were sent out together. Barnabas and Mark went together. Paul and Silas went together.

There were instances where Paul went alone but realized he needed help:

> The brothers immediately sent Paul to the coast, but Silas and Timothy stayed at Berea. The men who escorted Paul

brought him to Athens and then left *with instructions for Silas and Timothy to join him as soon as possible.* (Acts 17:14–15)

When Silas and Timothy came from Macedonia, Paul devoted himself exclusively to preaching, testifying to the Jews that Jesus was the Christ. (Acts 18:5)

Now when I went to Troas to preach the gospel of Christ and found that the Lord had opened a door for me, I still had no peace of mind, *because I did not find my brother Titus* there. So I said good-by to them and went on to Macedonia. (2 Cor. 2:12–13)

Paul had an open door. He did not take it because he had no one with him.

For when we came into Macedonia, this body of ours had no rest, but we were harassed at every turn—conflicts on the outside, fears within. *But God, who comforts the downcast, comforted us by the coming of Titus*, and not only by his coming but also by the comfort you had given him. He told us about your longing for me, your deep sorrow, your ardent concern for me, so that my joy was greater than ever. (2 Cor. 7:5–7)

It is much better to preach the gospel in pairs at least.

CONCENTRATED PRAYERS FOR EVANGELISM

Paul taught the efficacy of prayer especially for preaching the gospel and commanded the churches at Ephesus, Colossae, and Thessalonica to pray. Here are the commands:

And pray in the Spirit on all occasions with all kinds of prayers and requests. With this in mind, be alert and always keep on praying for all the saints.

Pray also for me, that whenever I open my mouth, words may be given me so that I will fearlessly make known the mystery of the gospel, for which I am an ambassador in chains. Pray that I may declare it fearlessly, as I should. (Eph. 6:18–20)

Devote yourselves to prayer, being watchful and thankful. *And pray for us, too, that God may open a door for our message, so that we may proclaim the mystery of Christ, for which I am in chains. Pray that I may proclaim it clearly, as I should.* (Col. 4:2–4)

Finally, brothers, *pray for us that the message of the Lord may spread rapidly and be honored*, just as it was with you. And pray that we may be delivered from wicked and evil men, for not everyone has faith. (2 Thess. 3:1–2)

Paul urged the Roman brothers to pray as well:

I urge you, brothers, by our Lord Jesus Christ and by the love of the Spirit, to join me in my struggle *by praying to God for me.* (Rom. 15:30)

CHAPTER 4

MOBILITY

The key communicator of the gospel is the saved man. He is alive with the Holy Spirit. He has access to unlimited amounts of Bibles, books, tracts, videos, CDs, the Internet, television, radio, cell phones, postal services, airplanes, ships, trains, buses, automobiles, horses, and wagons. He has the ability to go from his hometown to the uttermost parts of the earth, whether personally or electronically. He is not hampered. It no longer takes three months to get to India. Many saved people travel much and communicate much, but they do not preach the Gospel everywhere they go, as they go. They have mobility, but they do not use it for the kingdom.

Every Christian should have books, booklets, tracts, CDs, New Testaments and New Testament portions in English—or any other languages which people he is around speak—in his possession or within easy access at all times. Have them with you on the plane, in the hospital, in restaurants, in jail, etc.

In the weeks just prior to writing this I was away from home. On planes, in airports, restaurants, and in private meetings I had the right piece of literature for the right person in English, Spanish, and Chinese. In every case they were glad or very glad to receive it.

There are many positive effects of giving a book: It is a gift. People are grateful to receive it.

Books are considered authoritative.

Books are written on many subjects by many experts, all of whom know more than I do and express it better. They are also in many languages.

People can read the books while I am at home in bed. In other words, the books can do more evangelizing than I personally can.

If I give the person the right book for him, his esteem for me increases because of my love for him and for my wisdom in knowing his need.

My witness is magnified in quantity, in quality, in knowledge, in languages, in time, and in respect for me.

You can get a supply in any Christian bookstore, used bookstores, online, garage sales, or from the International Bible Society, the American Bible Society, or Multi-Language Media.

CHAPTER 5

SECURITY

INTELLIGENCE OF THE ENEMY

There is no question whether we are at war. We are. There is limited thinking among evangelicals about spiritual war. They mostly picture it as fighting with demons, devils, and evil spirits, either in possessed people or in the heavenlies. These things are a concern, but they are not what the war is really about. This war is over the souls of men. That is what the Bible, the gospel, the Incarnation, and the cross are all about. Evangelism is a war against the enemy to set free those who are held captive by him. Ignorance of the enemy is one of the reasons why evangelism is not effective.

The Bible gives some very clear information about the Enemy. Jesus said,

> You belong to your father, the devil, and you want to carry out your father's desire. He was a murderer from the beginning, not holding to the truth, for there is no truth in him. When he lies, he speaks his native language, for he is a liar and the father of lies. (Jn. 8:44)

He is a murderer from the beginning. There is no truth in
him. He is a liar; in fact, lying is his native language. He is
the father of lies.

> Yet because I tell the truth, you do not believe me! . . . He
> who belongs to God hears what God says. The reason you do
> not hear is that you do not belong to God. (Jn. 8:45,47)

Satan has children who are like him. Satan's children cannot
hear or believe the truth.

> For such men are false apostles, deceitful workmen, mas-
> querading as apostles of Christ. And no wonder, for *Satan*
> himself masquerades as an angel of light. (2 Cor. 11:13–14)

He masquerades as an angel of light.

> It is not surprising, then, if his servants masquerade as ser-
> vants of righteousness. Their end will be what their actions
> deserve. (2 Cor. 11:15)

His servants masquerade as servants of righteousness.

> And the Lord's servant must not quarrel; instead, he must
> be kind to everyone, able to teach, not resentful. Those who
> oppose him he must gently instruct, in the hope that God
> will grant them repentance leading them to a knowledge of
> the truth, and that they will come to their senses and escape
> from the trap of the devil, who has taken them captive to do
> his will. (2 Tim. 2:24–26)

Unbelievers are in the trap of the devil; he has taken them
captive to do his will.

> The god of this age has blinded the minds of unbelievers, so
> that they cannot see the light of the gospel of the glory of
> Christ, who is the image of God. (2 Cor. 4:4)

The devil is the god of this age. He blinds the minds of unbelievers so they cannot see the light of the gospel.

> No, we speak of God's secret wisdom, a wisdom that has been hidden and that God destined for our glory before time began. None of the rulers of this age understood it, for if they had, they would not have crucified the Lord of glory. (1 Cor. 2:7–8)

He does not understand God's secret wisdom.

> If you forgive anyone, I also forgive him. And what I have forgiven—if there was anything to forgive—I have forgiven in the sight of Christ for your sake, in order that *Satan* might not outwit us. *For we are not unaware of his schemes.* (2 Cor. 2:10–11)

> Put on the full armor of God so that you can take your stand against the devil's schemes. (Eph. 6:11)

We are to put on the full armor of God so we can stand against the devil's schemes. Because we are aware of those schemes, he is not able to outwit us.

> Be self-controlled and alert. Your enemy the *devil* prowls around like a roaring lion looking for someone to devour. (1 Pet. 5:8)

We are to be alert because the devil is looking for someone to devour.

> As for you, you were dead in your transgressions and sins, in which you used to live when you followed the ways of this world and of the *ruler of the kingdom of the air, the spirit who is now at work in those who are disobedient.* All of us also lived among them at one time, gratifying the cravings of our sin-

ful nature and following its desires and thoughts. Like the
rest, we were by nature objects of wrath. (Eph. 2:1–3)

He is the ruler of the ways of the world. We were under his
control before we were saved by grace.

He must not be a recent convert, or he may become conceited
and fall under the same judgment as the *devil*. (1 Tim. 3:6)

The devil is proud.

ENEMY ON THE OFFENSE

In the First World War, there were trenches from Switzer-
land to the English Channel. These trenches were called
the front lines, and it was there that the battles were fought.
There were also front lines in World War II, but they were
not as stationary. War today ignores front lines because of
missiles, air bombardment, guerillas, and terrorists. Both
sides fighting in the spiritual war also ignore lines (unless you consider every home, every vocation, every church,
school, and college in every nation a front line).

The Enemy is on the offense in all of these places all of
the time. His offense is through lying, stealing, rape, murder,
and war.

I know that after I leave, savage wolves will come in among
you and will not spare the flock. Even from your own number men will arise and distort the truth in order to draw away
disciples after them. So be on your guard! Remember that for
three years I never stopped warning each of you night and
day with tears. (Acts 20:29–31)

But there were also false prophets among the people, just
as there will be false teachers among you. They will secretly
introduce destructive heresies, even denying the sovereign

Lord who bought them—bringing swift destruction on themselves. Many will follow their shameful ways and will bring the way of truth into disrepute. In their greed these teachers will exploit you with stories they have made up. Their condemnation has long been hanging over them, and their destruction has not been sleeping. (2 Peter 2:1–3)

Then Peter said, "Ananias, how is it that Satan has so filled your heart that you have lied to the Holy Spirit and have kept for yourself some of the money you received for the land?" (Acts 5:3)

Jesus turned and said to Peter, "Get behind me, Satan! You are a stumbling block to me; you do not have in mind the things of God, but the things of men." (Mt. 16:23)

Be self-controlled and alert. Your enemy the devil prowls around like a roaring lion looking for someone to devour. (1 Pet. 5:8)

We have overcome our enemies:

You, dear children, are from God and have overcome them, because the one who is in you is greater than the one who is in the world. (1 Jn. 4:4)

CONTINUAL PROTECTION AGAINST THE ENEMY

Although we should take up the offense against the Enemy, we must also be able to defend ourselves against his attacks and counterattacks.

The more effective we are in our attack with the gospel, the more we will be counter-attacked. People who are in-effective with the gospel are not usually the ones who get martyred.

In fact, everyone who wants to live a godly life in Christ
Jesus will be persecuted. (2 Tim. 3:12)

Finally, be strong in the Lord and in his mighty power. Put
on the full armor of God so that you can take your stand
against the devil's schemes. For our struggle is not against
flesh and blood, but against the rulers, against the authorities,
against the powers of this dark world and against the spiritual forces of evil in the heavenly realms. Therefore put on the
full armor of God, so that when the day of evil comes, you
may be able to stand your ground, and after you have done
everything, to stand. Stand firm then, with the belt of truth
buckled around your waist, with the breastplate of righteousness in place, and with your feet fitted with the readiness that
comes from the gospel of peace. (Eph. 6:10–15)

Be self-controlled and alert. Your enemy the devil prowls
around like a roaring lion looking for someone to devour.
Resist him, standing firm in the faith, because you know that
your brothers throughout the world are undergoing the same
kind of sufferings. (1 Pet. 5:8–9)

At the same time, the Enemy has no effective defense
against our offense.

Submit yourselves, then, to God. *Resist* the devil, and he will
flee from you. (Jas. 4:7)

Resist him, standing firm in the faith, because you know that
your brothers throughout the world are undergoing the same
kind of sufferings. (1 Pet. 5:9)

The church of Christ has been ordered and equipped, in
order that she might take the offensive in every part of the
world through praying, preaching, and love. This offensive
includes evangelism everywhere by every believer.

But there have been many instances when the Church as a whole has not taken this offensive. It has been sleeping or on the defensive. Consequently, our homes, churches, cities, schools, and colleges have been taken over by the Enemy.

SATAN IS LIMITED

Since the great battle, the crucifixion and resurrection of Jesus Christ, the Enemy of our souls has been severely handicapped:

His power is limited.

> But *he was not strong enough*, and they lost their place in heaven. The great dragon was hurled down—that ancient serpent called the devil, or Satan, who leads the whole world astray. He was hurled to the earth, and his angels with him. (Rev. 12:8–9)

His intelligence is limited.

> No, we speak of God's secret wisdom, a wisdom that has been hidden and that God destined for our glory before time began. *None of the rulers of this age understood it,* for if they had, they would not have crucified the Lord of glory. (1 Cor. 2:7–8)

His time is limited, and he knows it.

> Therefore rejoice, you heavens and you who dwell in them! But woe to the earth and the sea, because the devil has gone down to you! He is filled with fury, for he knows that *his time is short.* (Rev. 12:12)

Yet his arrogance is unlimited.

> How you have fallen from heaven, O morning star, son of the dawn! You have been cast down to the earth, you who

once laid low the nations! You said in your heart, "I will ascend to heaven; I will raise my throne above the stars of God; I will sit enthroned on the mount of assembly, on the utmost heights of the sacred mountain. I will ascend above the tops of the clouds; *I will make myself like the Most High.*" (Is. 14:12–14)

We should know of Satan's limitations. We should remember that he is limited and not be intimidated as if Satan had omnipotent power.

So why are so many Christians defeated?

- They are unaware of the devil's schemes and his character.
- They have not put on their complete armor.
- They believe Satan or his ministers.
- They are not alert and self-controlled.
- They think it is normal to sin.
- They do not think that they have been delivered from the power of Satan.

Now get up and stand on your feet. I have appeared to you to appoint you as a servant and as a witness of what you have seen of me and what I will show you. I will rescue you from your own people and from the Gentiles. I am sending you to them to open their eyes and *turn them from darkness to light,* and *from the power of Satan to God,* so that they may receive forgiveness of sins and a place among those who are sanctified by faith in me. (Acts 26:16–18)

CHAPTER 6

COMMUNICATION

Communication is the logistic supply line that exists to get food, ammunition, and aid to the troops on the front lines. If the supply lines are cut off, the army will be defeated.

In the spiritual war of evangelism, everyone is on the front lines all the time. The supply line is keeping daily, hourly in fellowship with God by prayer and the word of God. Extra cover is provided by other people praying for you. If our line with the Lord is cut, we are going to be defeated.

There are several ways to stay in the Word of God:

Reading through the entire Bible (not just now and then and here and there). If you have read it through, read it again.[1]

---

1. If you would like a plan to help you read through the New Testament, you may send to Community Christian Ministries for the pamphlet *Read the New Testament in 67 Days* which lays out which chapters to read each day.

Study: "Do your best to present yourself to God as one approved, a workman who does not need to be ashamed and who correctly handles the word of truth" (2 Tim. 2:15). Study is always preceded by reading. The best study is re-reading. For example, read Ephesians 1–6 every day for a week. Then your study is contextual. It reinforces what you read yesterday, and you see something new each day.

Memorization: "I have hidden your word in my heart that I might not sin against you" (Ps. 119:11). Stephen preached before he was martyred. Read Acts 7. Stephen knew the Scriptures very well; he preached from memorized Scripture. If we are to preach the word of God, we must know it.

Listen to preaching: "Now the Bereans were of more noble character than the Thessalonians, for they received the message with great eagerness and examined the Scriptures every day to see if what Paul said was true" (Acts 17:11).

Meditation: "Blessed is the man who walks not in the counsel of the wicked, nor stands in the way of sinners, nor sits in the seat of scoffers; but his delight is in the law of the LORD, and on his law he *meditates* day and night. He is like a tree planted by streams of water that yields its fruit in its season, and its leaf does not wither. In all that he does, he prospers" (Ps. 1:1–3 ESV).

Preaching: "In the presence of God and of Christ Jesus, who will judge the living and the dead, and in view of his appearing and his kingdom, I give you this charge: *Preach the Word*; be prepared in season and out of season; correct, rebuke and encourage—with great patience and careful instruction" (2 Tim. 4:1–2). "Consequently, faith comes from hearing the message, and the message is heard through the word of Christ" (Rom. 10:17).

CHAPTER 7

ECONOMY OF FORCE

Unfortunately, the Christian church has frequently violated this principle. As I said in the chapter on concentration, it is important to send out men in twos. In this country, we have fallen into the trap of thinking that big is good, bigger is better, and biggest is best. So we have megachurches. In place of two-to-one concentration, we have six hundred-to-one or six thousand-to-one. This is not effective evangelism. It is not economy of force.

We have no idea how big the church in Jerusalem was, but it had five thousand men in Acts four. This did not include women and children.

> Nevertheless, more and more men and women believed in the Lord and were added to their number. (Acts 5:14)

> So the word of God spread. The number of disciples in Jerusalem increased rapidly, and a large number of priests became obedient to the faith. (Acts 6:7)

So this church was a mega-church. It met in Solomon's colonnade. What happened to it?

> On that day a great persecution broke out against the church at Jerusalem, and all except the apostles were scattered throughout Judea and Samaria . . . Those who had been scattered preached the word wherever they went. (Acts 8:1b, 4)

This was economy of force. The saints dispersed, and *all* of them preached the word everywhere they went.

We like to be together. But here is a sobering quotation from Ezekiel 33:30–32:

> As for you, son of man, your countrymen are talking together about you by the walls and at the doors of the houses, saying to each other, "Come and hear the message that has come from the LORD." My people come to you, as they usually do, and sit before you to listen to your words, but they do not put them into practice. With their mouths they express devotion, but their hearts are greedy for unjust gain. Indeed, to them you are nothing more than one who sings love songs with a beautiful voice and plays an instrument well, for they hear your words but do not put them into practice.

In many churches today the preacher is like the men in Ezekiel: good, clean entertainment for a Sunday morning.

To win the war in evangelism we must not over-concentrate. It is a waste of power. The saints with the gospel need to have more contact with the world. You do not have to be trained to be an evangelist. You only need to be saved and unashamed.

CHAPTER 8

TACTICAL SURPRISE

Tactical surprise is where a small group or a single person is caught by surprise. The object of surprise is to catch the listener with his guard down. We do not want to warn him that he is going to get hit.

It was December 31, 1949. I was in my senior year at the Naval Academy. I had been invited to give my testimony at an evangelistic dinner at the roof garden of the Hotel Astor in New York City. I gave my testimony and went back to my table. Jack Wyrtzen, the evangelist, was preaching the gospel when a note was handed to me from across the table. It said, "If you look behind you at the next table there is a sailor. I am his sister sitting next to him. When Jack gives the invitation to receive Christ will you encourage my brother to receive Christ?" When the invitation was given, I turned around and started to talk to the sailor. He was obviously ready. He was convicted, he believed, but he *would not* call upon the Lord. I pressured him. I got him to talk with the members of the quartet who had sung that evening. He still would not receive Christ. Against his will, I got him to talk with Jack Wyrtzen.

Jack said, "Glad to know you, Frank," and followed that up with, "What ship are you on? Where is your home town? Do you have a girlfriend?"

Frank was so glad to be talking about his ship, his home town, and his girl instead of Jesus Christ that he dropped his guard. In the middle of this, Jack grabbed him by the neckerchief and said, "Frank, what do you have against the Lord Jesus Christ?"

Frank fell apart and received the Lord. That was an example of tactical surprise. You should not necessarily copy it, but should see the principle involved and copy *that*. Pray for opportunities to use surprise.

The defender must be kept ignorant of what you are going to do or say. You must also be led by the Spirit in what you do and say.

Years ago I went to see a man who was divorcing his wife for another woman. He had his guard high. I said to him, "Do you think there is such a thing as a real Christian? A Christian from God's point of view?"

He was surprised at the question. He said yes.

"Are you one of them?"

He said yes again. Our conversation continued in a very open way. He dropped his guard when I opened the conversation in a way he did not expect. Surprise is a good thing. Use it.

CHAPTER 9

COOPERATION

Cooperation is working together with other units in the same army or with other nations against a common enemy. When we apply it to the spiritual war, there are two much stronger terms for it: "love for the brothers" and "unity in the body." This love is a very strong witness to the lost.

LOVE FOR THE BROTHERS

> A new command I give you: Love one another. As I have loved you, so you must love one another. *By this all men will know that you are my disciples, if you love one another.* (Jn. 13:34–35)

This is a major issue in evangelism. When the unsaved man looks at the fighting between Christians or Christian churches, why would he think we were followers of Jesus? Or why would he want to be a follower of Him?

For we were all baptized by one Spirit into one body—whether Jews or Greeks, slave or free—and we were all given the one Spirit to drink. (1 Cor. 12:13)

As a prisoner for the Lord, then, I urge you to live a life worthy of the calling you have received. Be completely humble and gentle; be patient, bearing with one another in love. Make every effort to keep the unity of the Spirit through the bond of peace. There is one body and one Spirit—just as you were called to one hope when you were called—one Lord, one faith, one baptism; one God and Father of all, who is over all and through all and in all. (Eph. 4:1–6)

*If you do not love the brothers, fix that **before** you start evangelizing.*

UNITY

In reading different histories of World War II, we can learn how the British won the war, how the Americans won the war, how the tanks, submarines, destroyers, airborne divisions, bombers, etc., each won the war. We were all on the same team, but it was not always evident.

Unity is comprised of two things: primary loyalty to the supreme commander of all units and great love for all those who are under the supreme commander.

Think of this as an equilateral triangle. The two points at the ends of the base of the triangle represent two units: tanks and infantry. The apex represents the supreme commander. If the two units get far away from the supreme commander, the distance between the units themselves also gets greater. Likewise, the closer they are to the supreme commander, the closer they are to each other.

Here is Jesus' prayer for His army in John 17:20–21:

My prayer is not for them alone. *I pray also for those who will believe in Me through their message*, that all of them may be one, Father, just as You are in Me and I am in You. May they also be in us so that the world may believe that You have sent Me.

Jesus was praying for *us* who are Christians today. He was praying that we would be one with each other in the same way as the Father and the Son are one.

How are they one? *Just as you are in me and I am in you.* That is not competition, nor is it cooperation. It is much greater—it is interactive unity.

Why does Jesus pray this? *So that the world may believe that You have sent Me.* The greatest truth in the gospel is the deity of Jesus Christ, and our oneness is the way we communicate the truth of that deity to the world.

A new command I give you: Love one another. As I have loved you, so you must love one another. *By this all men will know that you are my disciples, if you love one another.* (Jn. 13:34–35)

We are not to be at war with other members of the body of Christ. We are not to be satisfied with co-belligerence, tolerance, cordiality, friendliness, or mere cooperation. All of these are less than the command to be *one* and to love one another. Jesus tells us to love other members of the body in the same way that He loved each member of that body. If we have that love for one another, all men will know we are followers of Jesus Christ.

Do not jump to the question, "How do we do it?" That is not a relevant question until you first want to obey, want to love, and *want* to be one with fellow Christians. The sins of sectarian factionalism must be confessed before you can begin to desire this oneness.

CHAPTER 10

GENERAL THOUGHTS

PRIORITIES

Cairo is dirty. It is a city of ten million people, many of them unemployed, and there is much poverty. Garbage is collected by fifty thousand people who recycle it and live on it. Many of these are little children.

Germany, on the other hand, is scrupulously clean. While I was there, I saw a truck with a mechanical brush scrubbing the white posts along the highway; then I saw a man scrubbing a stop sign.

In both of these countries, the spiritual darkness is oppressive. It forced me to modify my view that physical cleanliness was the result of being spiritually clean. I still think there is a relationship, but not one of direct cause-and-effect.

There seem to be two extremes concerning methods of evangelism:

1. Too much identification with the attitudes of the local church

2. Too little identification with the culture of the local
   people

Japan and Egypt are examples of the first. The church in
those countries has a survival mentality rather than an attitude of "give me this mountain" (Josh. 14:12). In Japan, the
culture is accepted as something the gospel cannot penetrate
except in little ways. In Egypt, fear of the Muslims and fear
of the government makes people hesitant to witness. When
missionaries identify too much with the local church, they
are also affected by these attitudes. Consequently, there are
relatively few conversions.

Secondly, many missionaries depend heavily on dispens-
ing the truth by mass literature distribution without taking
time to love the people. In an endeavor to reach the whole,
they take a shortcut. This truncates the truth by presenting
it without the power that is part of the gospel. They trade
quality for quantity, but there are few real conversions.

A biblical example of the power of the gospel mixed with
love is found in 1 Thessalonians 1:4–8:

> For we know, brothers loved by God, that He has chosen you,
> because our gospel came to you not simply with words, but
> also with power, with the Holy Spirit and with deep convic-
> tion. You know how we lived among you for your sake. You
> became imitators of us and of the Lord; in spite of severe
> suffering, you welcomed the message with the joy given by
> the Holy Spirit. And so you became a model to all the believ-
> ers in Macedonia and Achaia. The Lord's message rang out
> from you not only in Macedonia and Achaia—your faith in
> God has become known everywhere. Therefore we do not
> need to say anything about it.

I have had much fellowship with people in mission
work—everything from long-term missionaries involved in

solid church planting to hit-and-run evangelists. Their biggest problem was not the difference in method, but the difference in relationships, mostly within missions and within families. I visited missionary children in Japan, Korea, the Philippines, Thailand, and France, and found much bitterness towards parents. As a corollary to that bitterness, I also saw some rebellion.

Many mission boards and the missionaries they send out think that the Great Commission is primary, that it is more important than personal godliness and more important than loving time with their children. Many of them also consider an American cultural Christian education more important than keeping the children with the parents. These two false priorities cause many families to be unnecessarily separated.

CARING FOR CASUALTIES

War has casualties. Taking care of them brings them back into the fight. It also increases the morale of the entire fighting unit because everyone knows they might be the next casualty. There are three kinds of casualties in physical war:

- Casualties from training[1]
- Casualties from drunkenness, drugs, and venereal disease
- Casualties from enemy action

There is no basic training or advanced training in the spiritual war. The soldier is in combat as soon as he is saved.

1. For example, during World War II, more planes and pilots were lost in training than in combat.

In the spiritual war, drunkenness, drugs, venereal disease, and other kinds of immorality which do not result in complete physical disability still cause spiritual disability and prevent effective evangelism. These casualties are to be disciplined by the church so they will repent and come back into action.

> But now I am writing you that you must not associate with anyone who calls himself a brother but is sexually immoral or greedy, an idolater or a slanderer, a drunkard or a swindler. With such a man do not even eat. What business is it of mine to judge those outside the church? Are you not to judge those inside? (1 Cor. 5:11–12)

There are physical casualties from enemy action in the spiritual war. The first death for Christ that Scripture records was Stephen in Acts 7:59–60. The second was the Apostle James in Acts 12:2. There were more people killed in the twentieth century for believing in Jesus than the total of such deaths over the previous 1,900 years. However, death is not our main problem. The main problem is the *sin* casualties. Christians who are spiritually sick are poor witnesses for Jesus Christ.

In the early part of the Vietnam War, I visited an officer at Walter Reed Army Hospital. He had been badly burned when his jeep hit a land mine. A Vietnamese soldier who was with him was also critically injured.

These two men were fellow soldiers. However, when they became casualties, a great difference suddenly manifested itself. The American went to a U.S. hospital and made a full recovery. The Vietnamese went to a Vietnamese hospital, where he almost certainly died. My friend told me how thankful he was to be in the U.S. army instead of the

Vietnamese army. He had also been wounded in the Korean Conflict, so he knew what he was talking about.

The difference in that situation lay in the quality of care given to casualties. The American army put a priority on caring for casualties; the Vietnamese did not. In other wars, in other armies, there has been a still greater difference: no care at all! Casualties were left to die. Their deaths had a significant impact on the men who remained uninjured. They were not willing to risk themselves in combat when they knew nobody cared enough to rescue them if they were wounded.

The U.S. had to relearn that lesson the hard way with Navy pilots in the Southwest Pacific in early 1942. The Navy decided not to risk other planes and ships and the lives of more men for the rescue of one man if a pilot had to ditch because his plane was shot up or had run out of fuel. The decision was based on economy; but the morale of the pilots went down so far that the decision was soon reversed, and the next pilot in the water was rescued at the expense of several other planes. Rescue and care of casualties is given high priority in the U.S. Armed Forces.

After the First Battle of the Philippine Sea, Admiral Mitscher's decision to guide his Air Groups home by turning on all the searchlights on all the ships of Task Force 58 was one of the great morale (and *moral*) decisions of the Second World War. He risked the lives of thousands to save the lives of a few.

I personally observed the priority given to rescuing casualties during the Korean War when, for three years, the U.S. Navy kept minesweepers and a rescue destroyer in Wonsan Harbor, in spite of the fact that all of the land around the harbor was held by North Korea. We were stationed there to pick up pilots who were forced to ditch in the harbor.

We Christians are engaged in a spiritual war that is far greater than World War II. It includes all people and nations everywhere. We have learned much about the conduct of war on the spiritual plane. We have learned about evangelism; we have learned about training and what is called discipling, but we have not learned about caring for our casualties. We have not learned about caring because we do not care. We have been taught to spend our time with the faithful few, not with the unfaithful many. The faithful few are a delight to be with, so the *esprit de corps* is seemingly high. But outside this group the casualties are many, and we cannot keep hiding from them. I cannot exist comfortably in an army where the overwhelming majority of the casualties are being ignored. I cannot maintain high morale in such an army. Such morale would be fake. Purporting to have it under those conditions is blinding oneself to reality.

This is because Christians are more than just an army; we are a body.

> But God has combined the members of the body and has given greater honor to the parts that lacked it, so that there should be no division in the body, but that its parts should have equal concern for each other. *If one part suffers, every part suffers with it;* if one part is honored, every part rejoices with it. (1 Cor. 12:24b–26)

The healthy parts suffer, too, since they are part of the body. If they are not suffering and caring, it is either because they are not part of the body or because they themselves are not healthy.

The status of our spiritual army today looks bad, with many casualties and most of the rest not caring.

> Brothers, if someone is caught in a sin, you who are spiritual should restore him gently. But watch yourself, or you also may be tempted. Carry each other's burdens, and in this way you will fulfill the law of Christ. (Gal. 6:1–2)

There are at least two reasons for not caring for our casualties. First is the cost. If we commit ourselves to caring for a physical invalid, then we are attached. Our time is committed: we cannot forsake the ill person. We also anticipate that if we lovingly begin to care for a spiritual casualty, then we will be forever attached to him. If there is more than one invalid, all of our time will disappear. We are not willing for that to happen.

This thinking assumes that people will *stay invalids* when they are cared for. But if they are cared for in the right way, then they will not. Loving, gentle care restores them, and does so quite rapidly. They will soon cease to be casualties, and we can get back to the work of evangelism more effectively than before.

The second reason for not looking after casualties is our hesitancy to use spiritual judgment. The enemy has infiltrated the camp of the believers through a misapplication of this passage:

> Do not judge, or you too will be judged. For in the same way you judge others, you will be judged, and with the measure you use, it will be measured to you. (Mt. 7:1–2)

Christians regularly say to each other, "Judge not!" The consequence of this peer pressure (which in itself uses the Word of God in a judgmental fashion) is to paralyze and intimidate the caring believers so they do not look after the casualties. They are led to pretend these casualties are not really injured at all. The results are obvious. Matthew 7:3–5 gives the context of the "do not judge" teaching:

> Why do you look at the speck of sawdust in your brother's eye and pay no attention to the plank in your own eye? How can you say to your brother, "Let me take the speck out of your eye" when all the time there is a plank in your own eye? You hypocrite, first take the plank out of your own eye, and then you will see clearly to remove the speck from your brother's eye.

This passage commands us to get rid of sin in our lives so that we may remove the speck from our brother's eye. That is loving, gentle care for a casualty. "Judge not" is a teaching given to keep *unqualified* people from trying to care for casualties. People who would make the situation worse are not to participate in the care. Paul says, "You who are *spiritual*" (Gal. 6:1), you who have removed the plank, you who see clearly—you are able to judge. When Jesus said, "If any one of you is without sin, let him be the first to throw a stone at her" (Jn. 8:7), He was keeping unqualified men from taking care of casualties. Then He took care of her Himself: "Go now and leave your life of sin" (Jn. 8:11).

When we quote these verses to each other, we stop attempts to care for those who are hurting, because we all have planks in our eyes; we have all sinned. We are not fit to be surgeons.

But we are Christians. God has made it possible for us to *get rid of our planks*, to get rid of our past sin. He *expects* us to be spiritual. He *expects* us to get qualified to care.

I say this to shame you. Is it possible there is nobody among you wise enough to judge a dispute between believers? (1 Cor. 6:5)

We are required to care. We could come up with the same excuses as the religious men in the story of the Good Samaritan. The casualty was there and could not help himself. The same situation exists today, and Jesus, commending the Samaritan, said to the expert in the law: "Go and do likewise" (Lk. 10:37).

In almost every group of Christians, there are men or women who have become casualties. In many cases, a faithful church or a study group or an annual conference is the means of restoring those believers to full health and combat readiness. But there are situations where the wounds cannot wait for the conference. You who are spiritual should restore him gently. If you are not qualified, then call on someone who is. But do not do *nothing*.

BATTLE FATIGUE

God planned for normal fatigue when He put the lights out on earth every night. He also set one day aside out of every seven for additional rest.

Battle fatigue is extreme: long marches, little sleep, no Sabbath rest, fear, dying and dead comrades and enemies, separation from family, no showers, inadequate food, and maybe being defeated in battle or wounded. You might get relief in a rear echelon, or you might not. This is a fatigue beyond being tired and exhausted. Eight hours of sleep and a weekend of rest cannot cure this.

We are in a spiritual war here and now. This war brings battle fatigue just like other wars do. Some of the symptoms are the same. Missionaries come home burnt out, irritable, or with nervous breakdowns or marriage and family problems.

There is a major difference between the soldier in physical war and the soldier in the spiritual war. The first has battle fatigue because he has *obeyed* his commanding officer. The second has battle fatigue because he has *disobeyed*, often while thinking he was being obedient.

Some Christians are disobedient casualties, shot by the enemy. They are moral casualties, guilty of sins clearly forbidden by Scripture. These Christians know they are in sin.

Other Christian casualties think they are not in sin, but they are. These are the battle fatigue casualties. So how have they been disobedient?

They volunteer and think that is obedience. They say, "Here I am, I'm going," instead of, "Here I am, *send me*" (Is. 6:8b).

They use their own strength instead of God's:

> We proclaim Him, admonishing and teaching everyone with all wisdom, so that we may present everyone perfect in Christ. To this end I labor, struggling with all *His* energy, which so powerfully works in me. (Col. 1:28–29)

They do not get enough sleep. There may be times when it is not possible to get enough sleep or observe the Sabbath because of Kingdom work. During those times, we do not need to get fatigued.

> Do you not know? Have you not heard? The LORD is the everlasting God, the Creator of the ends of the earth. He will not grow tired or weary, and His understanding no one can fathom. *He gives strength to the weary and increases the power of the weak.* Even youths grow tired and weary, and young men stumble and fall; but those who hope in the LORD will renew their strength. They will soar on wings like eagles;

they will run and not grow weary, they will walk and not be faint. (Is. 40:28–31)

They do not take a Sabbath rest.

They respond to challenges. A challenge is not the voice of God, but a temptation from the enemy. Remember, the devil appears as an angel of light. We should be able to recognize him for who he is.

They think that the Great Commission is primary.

"Teacher, which is the greatest commandment in the Law?" Jesus replied: "Love the Lord your God with all your heart and with all your soul and with all your mind." This is the first and greatest commandment. And the second is like it: "Love your neighbor as yourself." (Mt. 22:36–39)

The Great Commission falls under the second greatest commandment. It is not the first.

They spend more time "doing" than "being."

The list could go on and on. Prolonged rest is part of the solution for battle fatigue in physical wars. Confession of sin is the immediate solution for the spiritual war. This must include confessing moral sins like lying *and* confessing as sin the things that we do to "help God out." Then we can begin to be obedient God's way.

CHAPTER 11

FATHER, SON,

and Holy Spirit

As you read the Bible, I trust you will see that the great purpose of the Father, the Son, and the Holy Spirit is the salvation of men and of all creation along with them. In this chapter I have included a few passages of Scripture that will draw your attention to this truth.

> This is good, and pleases God our Savior, who wants all men to be saved and to come to a knowledge of the truth. For there is one God and one mediator between God and men, the man Christ Jesus, who gave Himself as a ransom for all men—the testimony given in its proper time. (1 Tim. 2:3–6)

God is described as being our Savior and wanting *all men* to be saved and to come to a knowledge of the truth. Jesus Christ is described as the one mediator who gave Himself as a ransom for all men.

> For this reason, since the day we heard about you, we have not stopped praying for you and asking God to fill you with

the knowledge of His will through all spiritual wisdom and understanding. And we pray this in order that you may live a life worthy of the Lord and may please Him in every way: bearing fruit in every good work, growing in the knowledge of God, and joyfully giving thanks to the *Father*, who has qualified you to share in the inheritance of the saints in the kingdom of light. For *He has rescued us from the dominion of darkness and brought us into the kingdom of the Son He loves,* in whom we have redemption, the forgiveness of sins. (Col. 1:9–14)

The work of the Father in our salvation and the work of the Son in our salvation are both described here. The Father qualified us to share in the inheritance of the saints in the kingdom of light, rescued us from the dominion of darkness, and brought us into the kingdom of the Son He loves. In the Son, we have redemption, the forgiveness of sins.

He did not enter by means of the blood of goats and calves; but He entered the Most Holy Place once for all by His own blood, having obtained eternal redemption. (Heb. 9:12)

For the grace of God that brings salvation has appeared to all men. It teaches us to say 'No' to ungodliness and worldly passions, and to live self-controlled, upright and godly lives in this present age, while we wait for the blessed hope—the glorious appearing of our great God and Savior, Jesus Christ, who gave Himself for us to redeem us from all wickedness and to purify for Himself a people that are His very own, eager to do what is good. (Tit. 2:11–14)

This redemption is from all wickedness, and it is eternal.

The Holy Spirit gives that new birth without which we will not enter the Kingdom of God:

Jesus answered, "I tell you the truth, no one can enter the kingdom of God unless he is born of water and the Spirit. Flesh gives birth to flesh, but the Spirit gives birth to spirit. You should not be surprised at my saying, 'You must be born again.' The wind blows wherever it pleases. You hear its sound, but you cannot tell where it comes from or where it is going. So it is with everyone born of the Spirit." (Jn. 3:5–8)

CHAPTER 12

CONCLUSION

In the history of the world there have been successive empires, including the Assyrian, Babylonian, Persian, Grecian, Roman, Frankish, Mongolian, Muslim, Byzantine, Ottoman, Napoleonic and Nazi regimes. These had a few characteristics in common with each other:

1. Absolute authority
2. Required loyalty to the sovereign
3. Required absolute obedience

The leaders of these empires were not noted for humility, kindness, or love. Submission was largely out of a fear of the consequences. They used the weapons of this world. Although these men had great authority, their empires lasted an average of only 250 years (Napoleon's and Hitler's lasted much less).

Jesus said, *"All* authority in heaven and on earth has been given unto me" (Mt. 28:18). That is a lot of authority. He required obedience, *but not out of fear.* His leadership was one of love, humility, sacrifice, and spiritual power. Many of his followers have lived their lives and deaths in obedience to and imitation of Christ.

When an emperor gives a command, it is personally given to his generals. They in turn give it to all of their officers who give it to the common soldiers. In other words, the commander in chief's orders are to everyone, not just to the generals. The generals alone cannot accomplish the tasks assigned.

So it is with Jesus Christ's operational order. It does not apply to the apostles only. They could not do it all. Let us look at the grammar of the order:

> Then Jesus came to them and said, "All authority in heaven and on earth has been given to me. Therefore go and make disciples of all nations, baptizing them in the name of the Father and of the Son and of the Holy Spirit, and teaching them to obey everything I have commanded you. And surely I am with you always, to the very end of the age." (Mt. 28:18–20)

The first sentence is the basis for the command: make disciples of all nations. The second sentence begins with "therefore," meaning you have no reason to ignore or disobey the command to make disciples (recruiting soldiers for His army). Then He tells the apostles how to carry out this command:

1. Baptizing in the name of the Father, Son, and Holy Spirit
2. Teaching them to obey everything He commanded

Number one is conversion. Number two is the sanctification of the believer. Each believer is to make believers and teach them to obey everything the Eleven were commanded.

The Great Commission is to every Christian. If we are not participating in the evangelization of the world at some level, then we are being disobedient soldiers.

> Jesus said to him, "Today salvation has come to this house, because this man, too, is a son of Abraham. For the Son of Man came to seek and to save what was lost." (Lk. 19:9–10)

"We are forlorn like children, and experienced like old men, we are crude and sorrowful and superficial—I believe we are lost."[1]

The lostness of the lost! Unlike the soldier quoted above, the lost do not know they are lost. The saved also do not know, or if they do know, they do not care. If the saved do care, they either do not know how to help the lost or they are afraid to help.

---

1. Erich Maria Remarque, *All Quiet on the Western Front*, trans. A. W. Wheen (Boston: Little, Brown, 1929).

CPSIA information can be obtained at www.ICGtesting.com
Printed in the USA
BVOW082319051212

307377BV00005B/27/P